Dear Mr. Gillespie:

I'll Take My Psyche Back, If You Are Finished With It

J. Roger Smith

BOOK TITLE

ISBN : 9781530295074

This book is dedicated first of all to my stepmother Lisa, who passed away a month before publication. Secondly, it is dedicated to all my nieces and nephews. Besides the couple of them that I have mentioned in this book, there are over a dozen more. They may not have fit in my storyline, but they are all dear to my heart. Thirdly, this book is dedicated to my roommate Bob. If he had not provided me with a place to live and transportation to work over the past decade, I'm not sure where I would be today. This book would not be possible without his patience and generosity. Lastly, but most importantly, this book is dedicated to Jesus Christ. He is the Rock that has always been faithful throughout my rebellious life. He has always been there for me whenever I turned to Him. To Him be the power and glory and dominion forever.

Books by J. Roger Smith

Jonah's Hill (2015)

I Am... Jesus (2015)

A-nimal-Z (2016)

Intelligent Design: From Telescope to Microscope (Coming Soon)

Table of Contents

CHAPTER I

Demonic Domination

TO MAKE THE most sense out of what you have just now begun to read, I would like to take you back to the beginning. It was late in the summer of 1976. My sister Katy and I lived with our mother Becky. Becky was a short, thin, long-haired brunette with huge piercing blue eyes. It was an effortless task for anyone to read her emotions as her eyes seemed to broadcast each one in HD—Blue Ray, if you will.

Becky was twenty years old at the time and recently divorced from my father Tony, who was twenty-one. Tony was about an inch or two taller than my mother, with a thin build. Tony also had brown hair, about shoulder length, but his eyes were much smaller and brown. Tony was happily remarried; moreover, he was ecstatic as his new bride Lisa had just given birth to my brother, Thomas. Thomas was born with very little hair that was reddish brown. He had blue eyes.

My step-mother, Lisa, was a nineteen-year-old with long, flowing red hair and blue eyes. She had a fair complexion that was sporadically populated by freckles. Lisa already had a son from a previous marriage named Michael. Michael was only a year older than I, but quite a bit taller. He had blond hair and blue eyes.

At just three years old, I was already blessed with beautiful sister and a pair of wonderful brothers. We all hit it off right away. Michael, Katy, Thomas and I were always very close. To us, there was no such thing as a half or step sibling. We were just family.

My mother, Becky, was still single. Although she tried dating a few times, she often found herself extremely lonely. I was a happy-go-lucky three-year-old with curly blond hair and big blue eyes. Over the years, my blond hair gradually darkened to almost black.

I was the spitting image of my father with my mother's eyes. Katy was born with quite a bit of dark brown hair. She had brown eyes just like our father Tony.

Becky, Katy and I attended an independent Baptist church. Despite my young age, I would sit quietly next to my mother and listen to the sermons. My little sister Katy and the other children were in the church nursery during that time. Afterward, I always had a million questions for my mother regarding what I heard. I would ask her simple questions such as:

"If Jesus is with us right now, then why can't I see him?"

I would also ask her more difficult questions like:

"If God created two people who had only two sons, then where did all those other people come from that Cain was worried about?"

Becky always tried to answer my questions as best as she could, but my enquiries were often too in-depth. For these, she would refer me to Pastor Graves.

Pastor Graves was a tall, medium-built sixty-something-year-old with white hair that only partially covered his scalp. He also boasted a round face with an ever-present warm smile. Pastor Graves was always pleased to oblige Becky, as he was very much intrigued by my inquisitive nature.

One night I had a vision as I lay in my bed. I saw Satan at the foot of my bed reaching up towards me. He was dark red with horns, and he held a pitchfork in his left hand. He had a tail that looped over his left shoulder and ended in a spade-shaped tip.

I do not believe this is Satan's actual form. He is the *prince of darkness*, the *master of deceit* and the *father of lies*. He has the supernatural ability to change his appearance to fit into any situation to accomplish his goals. What better way to get the attention of a three-year-old than to appear to him this way?

Satan's appearance caused the air in my bedroom to become very hot and dry, with a musky odor. Immediately after Satan appeared to me, an angel appeared at the side of my bed, by my right shoulder. He had huge wings that arched well over his head. The wings were a bluish-white in color and radiated many brilliant colors. The angel reached out his hand toward me, and when I took it, Satan and the stench went away and the room became much cooler.

The angel helped me out of bed and escorted me to my mother's room a few steps away. When we reached her door, the angel disappeared. I woke my mother up and with tears in my eyes, I begged her to save me. That night I accepted Jesus Christ as my Lord and Savior.

The next Sunday, the sermon was about baptism. For several weeks afterward, I begged my mother to allow me to get baptized. Becky ignored me at first, but eventually my persistence tore down her reservations. Finally, my mother approached Pastor Graves about my request. He was initially hesitant as well.

About a year later, Pastor Graves would announce to the congregation:

"I don't normally baptize someone this short, but when I took this young man into my inner chambers and questioned him extensively, his testimony came out clear as a bell. As a result, I have decided that, in the event his wisdom is born of the Spirit, I will baptize him. I do not want to be in opposition to the Spirit!"

After each sermon, it was customary for everyone to shake hands and mingle for a bit in the church foyer. Becky had always taught me to respect my elders and to use the terms:

"Yes, sir" and "No, ma'am" wherever appropriate.

I recall many times while I was scurrying past the adults, my mother would grab me by my ear and scold me for not saying:

"Excuse, me."

Each time Becky would be told that I did say it, but she just didn't hear me.

One Sunday afternoon as everyone was doing their post sermon meet and greet routines, a family friend introduced Becky to a man named David Gillespie. David was a short, stocky, fair-skinned redhead with black wire-rimmed glasses. He was a twenty-six-year-old ex-cop who was currently the church's bus driver and deacon, among other things.

My mother fell for David almost immediately. David was the epitome of the lady's man: romantic, charming, and silver tongued. He took her to dinner quite a bit and even went as far as to take Katy and me to the St. Louis Zoo and to Six Flags.

My mother was struggling financially at the time, so these gestures were a breath of fresh air to her. David used to take me fishing as well. He called it:

"Doing the guy thing."

Tragically, fishing with him became an activity that I feared terribly.

On a cold winter evening in 1977, David proposed to my mother. Although their courtship was brief; Becky quickly accepted, as tears of joy streamed down her face. If Becky only knew that in a few short months, she'd be crying all the time—just not happy tears . . . The result of her decision to marry David Gillespie had a lasting effect on me.

Less than two months from the time he proposed to her, my mother married David Gillespie. The honeymoon did not last long. Everything quickly changed; almost from the very moment that Becky said:

"I do!"

The *lady's man* disappeared. In his stead was a quick-tempered, controlling, physically and mentally abusive womanizer.

A week after the marriage we moved into a bi-level, three-bedroom apartment in a subsidized district of town. In addition to his fondness for fishing, David was an avid deer hunter. He had a bow and an extensive collection of guns and rifles. David decided to convert the third bedroom of our new apartment into his workshop. He would store his hunting equipment there.

One evening while David was in his workshop cleaning his guns, one of them *accidently* went off. The round went through the wall of our apartment and into the bathroom of our neighbor's. Later, the woman from that apartment told my mother that her son was supposed to be brushing his teeth at the time, but he was fortunately downstairs arguing with her about it.

David shared his passion for deer hunting with a fellow church member named Terry Lansing. Terry was a tall, blond-haired, green-eyed man with broad shoulders and an athletic build. He was in his mid-twenties. As a gift to the newlyweds, Terry gave David a handcrafted, one-and-a-half inch thick paddle. This *gift* was to be used for corporal punishment, which David put to use on a regular basis.

David and Becky both worked third shift. One night I awoke and could hear the television playing downstairs. I got out of bed and slowly crept down the hallway. David met me halfway and told me that we need to go to his workshop,

'... because I have to be punished for getting out of bed'.

David kept the paddle there. He normally used the paddle on my bottom, and he did so this time. Although that was not always the case.

A couple of months later he was trying to teach me how to read. I excelled at:

"C-A-T."

and

"D-O-G."

So David got out my Fisher Price farm set. Above the white sliding door to the chicken coop was the Fisher Price logo. David became more and more frustrated with me because I was not pronouncing *Fisher* properly.

He picked up the paddle to "encourage" me, but his attempt was unsuccessful. Ultimately, my step father struck me in the side of the face with it, blackening my right eye and bruising my cheek. David did not seem to understand that *Fisher* was a complex word for a four-year-old to learn to read.

David insisted that I called him daddy and Superman. He attempted to prove to me that he was, in fact Superman; by pointing out that black glasses that he was wearing, were just like Clark

Kent's. He further emphasized his point by showing me his

bulletproof police vest. David explained that in real life Superman is

not bulletproof without it. From fear of punishment, I agreed with

him.

In the fall of 1978, I began kindergarten at Faith Baptist

Christian School. David convinced Becky to have *Gillespie* engraved

as my last name on my Bible. He also implored Becky to allow him

to adopt me. Luckily, my biological father Tony successfully

objected to the adoption.

We lived in the apartment for about a year and a half. One

night, just a few weeks before we moved; Becky was in the kitchen

preparing dinner. I was sitting at the table playing with my action

figures.

Suddenly, David came into the kitchen screaming at Becky.

He then began choking my mother and slapping her around. I tried to

run to my room, but David slammed me against the kitchen wall and

ground his head into my abdomen as he said:

"Where are you going, sissy?"

The assault on Becky carried over into the living room, where I managed to make it as far the recliner. At this point, David had my mother pinned to the floor as he continued to beat her. Becky screamed at me to go call the cops, but when I attempted to move from my seat, David, glared at me and shouted:

"Don't move!"

At this point I was paralyzed with fear, so I just sat there.

Not long after this, David accepted a better-paying job at an ice-cream factory. This job was also third shift. Still, the increase in income allowed us to rent a two-story, two-bedroom house located in a much-better area of town. We lived here for the remainder of the marriage.

David had a fondness for dressing me up in my sister's dresses while Becky wasn't home. He enjoyed dressing me up, taking me to the front porch and leaving me out there; locking the door behind him. I must have been quite a sight for the passing motorists, as I stood there wearing Katy's dresses with my short, tapered Baptist haircut. Besides calling me sissy from time to time, David also told me that I wasn't a little boy—I was a little girl!

For as long as I can remember, I have been nocturnal by nature. Because of this, I have always had the most difficult time getting to sleep at night. One evening about an hour after bedtime, I got out of my rack for about the third time.

After both screaming at me and later paddling me seemed to have no effect in correcting my behavior, David took me in the bathroom. He lifted up the porcelain toilet seat lid and made me put my penis on the rim below. David then slammed the lid down onto my member.

That weekend I was spending time at my father Tony's house. At bath time, my stepmother Lisa noticed that my penis was black and blue and swollen. She informed my father about the situation.

Tony asked me about it. Out of fear of a beating when I got back home, I made up excuses. I'm certain that Tony asked Becky about it as well; but to this day, I am not sure of the outcome of their conversation. It appears to be a topic that neither one is willing to discuss with me.

As I mentioned before, I was David's reluctant fishing companion. David's style of *manning me up* was to make me carry our tackle boxes while he searched for the right fishing spot. Because I was quite a small lad, the tackle boxes seemed to weigh as much as I did. As a result, they became quite heavy after a while. David was always getting angry with me because I wasn't keeping up with him while he walked.

On one occasion, he took one of the boxes out of my hand and told me I could rest for a minute if I needed to. I set the remaining box on the ground, and then I sat on it. David walked on ahead.

I sat there for what seemed like an eternity, dreading the moment when I would have to get up and eventually be around him again… Suddenly, I was startled out of my *day* mare by David's voice cursing and screaming at me from across the lake.

Aside from carrying the tackle boxes, I do not recall any other physical abuse from these trips. The potential for it; however, kept me in a constant state of fear. Thinking about what might happen made these fishing trips dreadful.

David liked to wrestle with me. He would start each match by yanking me by an arm and a leg off of the sofa and spinning me around very fast. He would then set me on the ground and lie on me. That was it; no wrestling moves. He would lie atop me for what seemed like hours, pinning my arms and legs beneath his body.

I never liked him spinning me around like that and to this day, I cannot sleep with my feet under the covers. It makes me feel pinned down, immobilized, and even trapped. Just the thought of it brings on an overwhelming feeling of helplessness.

Possibly from nerves, I was a sickly young man. One morning I was too sick to stand up. While David was carrying me down the stairs, I suddenly felt nauseous. Noticing this, David warned me:

"Don't dare!"

My vomit had already filled up my mouth at this point, but I swallowed it anyway. This was much better than facing the consequences of disobeying him.

Still another time I was so sick that I vomited in my bowl of cereal. David backhanded me with a closed fist, sending me sprawling across the floor. If this was not enough punishment for being sick, he then yanked me up and made me go stand in the corner with my arms raised to my sides.

The next time my mother went grocery shopping I begged her to take me with her. David interjected, telling me that shopping is a woman thing and that it's been a while since we've had any *father/son* time. My mother left me behind.

As soon as she was gone, David began asking me why I didn't like being alone with him. He asked me this over and over again, becoming increasingly more agitated at my lack of a reply. The terror of what might happen to me should I answer him incorrectly caused me to remain silent. Although my silence, itself, could have easily done its own damage.

16

Finally, David changed the subject. He said:

"Let's watch some TV. Would you like to watch a program about silver or gold?"

He was asking if I wanted to watch the *Lone Ranger*, referring to *Silver* the name of his horse, or a pirate movie. I knew this but, once again out of fear of giving him an unsatisfactory response, I remained silent. As punishment for not answering him, David locked me in the food pantry until my mother returned, hours later.

My mother went witnessing door to door, every Saturday afternoon with Mrs. Graves, our pastor's wife. Like her husband, Mrs. Graves was in her mid-sixties. She was a tall, strong-minded lady with a bit of an aristocratic aura about her. She wore bifocals that seemed to take up half of her face. Aside from her appearance, Mrs. Graves had a very kind and generous heart.

Soon after they left on one of their *crusades*, David told me it was time for my nap. I went up to my room and lay on my bed.

David entered my room and when he did my body instinctively stiffened up. My body did this whenever he approached me.

David came to my bedside and asked me why I was so nervous. He told me over and over again that I just needed to relax. Not finding any success from his efforts, David did the unthinkable.

He removed his pants and straddled my chest. He told me to open my mouth, and when I did, he inserted his penis. He told me to suck on it as he began to rock backward and forward.

This only lasted for a couple of minutes, but the memory has lasted my entire life.

Later, I told my mother about it. Becky reported the incident to our church leaders. I am still not sure why she did not go to the police about it.

The church elders questioned me about it, specifically asking me to describe David's penis to them. Later when our church leaders were discussing the situation again with Becky, they dismissed the accusation as the active imagination of a child. They declared that no mature man's penis could possibly be that small. Ashamed to admit that my description was accurate, my mother agreed with them.

Unfortunately, this was the turning point in our relationship with the church. The church leaders staunchly supported David in the matter while systematically holding my mother and me in contempt for bringing up false accusations. Mrs. Graves quit inviting my mother on Saturday witnessing outings, and it seemed like the entire church had turned a cold shoulder to Becky, Katy, and I.

At the same time, they went out of their ways to see to it that David continued to have their full support, even to the point of giving him a place to stay during the separation that resulted. Not long thereafter, Becky divorced him.

It would have been too lengthy and drawn out to relate every single thing that David Gillespie did to us here. Besides the ones that I have illustrated, there were countless more. He also directed his abuses toward my sister Katy.

Although the abuse ended long ago, its ghost has haunted me throughout the years since. David Gillespie's psychological, physical, and sexual abuses of me from the ages of four to six; have destroyed my self-esteem, retarded my sexual development/orientation, and made me overall paranoid about the intentions and motives of those around me. This has ultimately denied me the ability to maintain any meaningful interpersonal relationship, whether friendly or intimate. In a relatively short amount of time, David Gillespie raped me of my psyche. What follows is my impression of how that rape affected my intimate relationships, career and social life throughout the ensuing years.

CHAPTER II

From Christianity to Secularism

ALTHOUGH OUR RELATIONSHIP with the church had been permanently scarred after the Gillespie incident, my mother continued to enroll me in its school system for a few years. As I began first grade at the Christian school, my mother started dating a man named Kenny Wilson. She was pregnant at the time with David Gillespie's baby, but Kenny didn't seem to mind at all.

Kenny worked as a maintenance man at a local restaurant. This was a job that he managed to keep for many years to come. Kenny was a thin, but muscularly built man of average height. He was of medium complexion, sporting long brown hair and hazel eyes.

Kenny was a year or two older than my mother. His looks reminded me of Burt Reynolds. At first he was energetic and a lot of fun to be around, but still I was mistrusting.

Kenny took us camping all the time and even tried fishing with us as well. He quickly observed that my mother wasn't much of a fisherman and that I wasn't interested in the prospect at all. Kenny simply tossed the poles aside and asked:

"Who wants to go swimming?"

Becky, Katy, and I jumped at the chance. We couldn't get our bathing suits on quick enough!

The water was dark, but I could feel the tickling sensation as the sand on the bottom worked its way between my toes. I noticed if I walked too far from shore in a certain spot, the water would creep closer and closer toward my neck.

A little while later, I heard my mother's voice calling to me. I looked to see where the voice was coming from and was shocked to see Kenny, Becky and Katy almost halfway to the other side of the lake!

Kenny motioned for me to join them, but I refused. I had not learned how to swim yet. I told him that the water was too deep out there. My mother was holding Katy at the time, so she set her down.

Katy, about a head and a half shorter than I, simply smiled and waved at me. I still refused and insisted that they were holding my sister up. I didn't trust Kenny and sadly, for that matter, I must not have trusted my mother either. I guess that subconsciously I held her in contempt for leaving me alone with David Gillespie all those times.

Kenny liked to wrestle with me as well. At first I was hesitant. Kenny's style of wrestling was a lot different than David Gillespie's. Kenny liked to do a lot of tickling. He always let me believe that I had the upper hand. I slowly began to enjoy these matches.

Not long after this, Underoos came on the market. They were a T-shirt and underwear line that specialized in superhero costumes. Between my mother and my father, I believe that I owned the entire lineup.

Many times after this Kenny would appear to be winning our wrestling matches, but I would somehow manage to escape his clutches long enough to retreat to my bedroom. I would return moments later in costume. It didn't matter if I was now the Hulk, Superman, or Batman. Kenny knew that he was in for a whooping at this point! During this time, I have to admit that I did have a lot of fun with Kenny. I was still mistrusting though; after all, he was not my dad.

Tony had joint custody of Katy and me for quite a while at this point. We were allowed to spend every other weekend at his house, as well as two weeks every summer. Although we did manage to visit him many times, there were far too many memories of crying myself to sleep on my packed suitcase.

Later, my mother would gently wake me up and put me in my bed, because my father didn't show up. There was also many times where Tony would pick me up but not my sister. This is another topic that my parents do not discuss.

I recall a memorable visit to my father's house when I was five or six years old. On Saturday afternoon my stepmother Lisa had us lie down for a nap. Soon afterward I started itching all over and I also began to have trouble breathing. Lisa was lying on the couch attempting a nap of her own.

I walked over to the couch where she was lying with her back to me. I tapped her on her shoulder. Without turning around my stepmother said:

"I told you to go lie down!"

I tapped her on the shoulder again. Lisa angrily turned around. However, she quickly changed her expression to one of fear and deep concern. I stood there in front of her with my face bright red and my lips, neck and cheeks swollen to twice their normal sizes. Lisa took me in her arms and screamed for my father. Tony came running and we went straight to the emergency room.

As it turned out I had been bitten by a spider. The doctor who treated me could not determine what species of spider had done the damage. He only said that, based on my condition when I arrived, I had an acute allergy to spider bites.

The doctor gave me a couple of immunizations and an I.V. which returned my body to normal. A couple of hours later I went home with a handful of lollipops. To this day I always kill a spider if I see it in the house. I do not take any chances on it biting me later.

About two months before my mother was due to have her baby, Kenny proposed to her. Becky accepted, and even I was happy about it. A month later, to the surprise of us all, little Brooke introduced herself to the world a few weeks early! Kenny was there holding Becky's hand the entire time.

Kenny and Becky decided to go ahead and push the wedding date up; so with Brooke barely a month old, they made it happen. It was a happy ceremony that I took very seriously. Katy was the flower girl, while I was in charge of the rings. There is a photograph of me frowning and glaring at Katy as I escorted her down the aisle because she was giggling. The reception was modest, but a lot of fun, with quite a bit of dancing and singing.

This was the summer of 1980. Before the summer was half through, Kenny adopted Brooke. That fall I would be starting the third grade.

This would turn out to be my final year at Faith Baptist Christian School. Every year the tuition costs skyrocketed. Kenny was a hard worker, but his income was meager and Becky struggled to balance taking night courses and raising three kids.

Becky had quite a temper. I'm not sure if it was from repressed guilt of our time with David Gillespie, memories from her childhood or financial frustrations. She sure could fly off the handle quickly though.

She was always making Katy or me; either scratch her back or brush her hair. She would expect us to do this way beyond the time that our wrists became tired. If we stopped for even a second, she would first warn us, and then strike us—with the brush if it was available.

One October morning on school picture day, Becky was reviewing my report card. She was unhappy with my marks so she threw the report card at me and left a mark of her own—underneath my left eye. Unfortunately, that didn't turn out to be my best school picture.

Meanwhile, life with Kenny also had its ups and downs. Married life turned Kenny into a chronic procrastinator and an extreme pessimist. He was most often found sitting in his favorite chair in front of the television set, next to an ashtray overflowing with cigarette butts and sporting his ever-present frown. He always had to be in control of the situation. Looking back, I realize this was not the case for Kenny at work. All those years of making next to nothing at the restaurant and having even less to show for it, must have made him a very frustrated man at his castle.

In spite of his shortcomings, Kenny meant well. He assisted with the activities of daily living. He even took a proactive approach toward homework tutoring. The latter turned out to be a problem as academics were not Kenny's forte.

At first, the mathematics, spelling and punctuation were easy for him to instruct. It did not take me very long, however, to solve the equations and finish the sentences before he did. This frustrated Kenny even more.

He and I shared a love for board games. Stratego, a particular board game, was one that Kenny always seemed to beat me at. The only time that I was successful, he was not happy. Kenny took his open palm and slapped the remaining tokens off of the board and on to the floor. He then sat there quietly and sulked. I was happy with my achievement for only a moment. I began to think, as much as I hate to lose, winning isn't that special either. I have never played that game again.

Kenny also was active in our discipline, fortunately, not to the degree of Gillespie. During one of my tantrums, I stormed off to my room, shoving the door open forcefully with my palms. Kenny was behind me and on top of me before the door could close on its own.

While I admit that this was not like my wrestling matches with Gillespie, I still recall the feeling of being pinned down and helpless.

This would not be the last time that Kenny and I got physical, only the last time that I would lose.

Kenny continued to pursue the ritual of going fishing, just he and I at this point, but no matter how much effort that he put into it, I wasn't biting. I had no problem baiting my own hook or anything; I was just more interested in throwing rocks and splashing my feet in the water. These behaviors had a negative effect on Kenny. He was always yelling at me that I was scaring off all the fish.

Sadly, due to my prior experiences of fishing with a stepdad; Kenny's aspiration of bonding with me, doing something that he enjoyed, failed. Later, it must have been a blow to Kenny's self-esteem when my Uncle Bob began taking me fishing. I always came home excited about our trips, usually sporting a bucket full of blue gills.

My Uncle Bob and his wife, Aunt Mary, were a stabilizing force in my tumulus childhood. I was actually their great-nephew. They raised my mother and her own siblings throughout most of their childhoods because their father was abusive and their mother was an alcoholic.

Besides going fishing with Uncle Bob, I spent the night at his house all the time with my cousin. While we were there we enjoyed playing Whiffle Ball and video games. We also enjoyed eating butter pecan ice cream. This was also Uncle Bob's favorite flavor.

Many times an overnight visit would last three or four days. I would simply call my mother and ask her to let me stay another day. Uncle Bob never grew tired of our visits.

Uncle Bob was a World War II veteran who was also retired from the railroad. He was medium height and heavyset. He had black hair and brown eyes and had a dark complexion.

Aunt Mary worked as the secretary for a major car dealership. Her dresser was always adorned with half a dozen wigs. Her real hair was gray, and she had blue eyes. She was short, heavyset, and had a light complexion.

Oddly enough, I do not recall them ever showing any affection towards one another. Aunt Mary would sit in her recliner across the room from Uncle Bob. He would lie on the sofa next to one of their three poodles. Every evening they would sit like this cursing at each other and trading insults.

They each had their own bedroom as well. The only time I saw Uncle Bob show any emotion was at Aunt Mary's funeral in 2003. She died of lung cancer, and sadly, he succumbed to colon cancer himself four years later.

One other source of escape for me came in the form of my best friend growing up. His name was Brett Rivers. Brett was a year older than me. He had very curly sandy blond hair, a light complexion and a thin build.

His mother Tina was also my mother's best friend. Tina was just a few years older than my mother with long blond hair and hazel eyes. She was short with a slightly voluptuous build. On many occasions while my mother was still married to David Gillespie, she would drop Katy and me off at Tina's house when things got out of control at our own home.

Brett and I had a lot of common interests; among them, *Star Wars* and wrestling. Every time we spent the night together, we would spend the evening recreating the scenes from the movie verbatim. We also did a lot of wrestling, of course. Whenever one of these visits was over though, I felt emptiness deep inside. I felt alone and depressed.

After I completed the third grade, my mother took Katy and me out of Faith Baptist and enrolled us in the public school system. Up until this point I had always been on the honor roll. As I began the fourth grade I did not know anyone, but I tried really hard to fit in.

That year a television program called the *A-team* began airing on Tuesday nights on a local channel. It was about a renegade commando unit of four for hire in the Los Angeles underground. Three of my new classmates and I began playing as the *A-team* at recess. One of the four characters was an insane man. I played this role.

Trying to fit in, I took the insane role to the extreme. If the character of my inspiration talked to imaginary animals, then I would talk to imaginary animals. If he wore a sock puppet on his left hand and carried on conversations with it, then I would do likewise.

One day my teacher read us a children's story. One of the characters in the story ate some worms as a prank. That afternoon in the school yard, I attempted it. This stunt would come back to haunt me time and time again through my first year of high school.

In my efforts to be accepted I was actually isolating myself. In junior high I couldn't get a date for a dance, or even one dance, for that matter. Who would have wanted to get caught dancing with the worm eater?

In spite of my self-inflicted general isolation, I did manage to make a few friends. These friends taught me that it was okay to curse, so long as we didn't get caught. It was cool to ditch class every once in a while.

I was effectively becoming more and more rebellious. I stopped doing my homework on a regular basis, and when I did go to class, I was disruptive and had to make several trips to the principal's office, all in my naïve attempt at being popular.

While I was in the fifth grade my sister Katy and I decided it would be pretty cool to run away. We had talked about it many times before. We would run away to the prairie leaving all our problems behind. I would build us a log cabin, and we would live off the land.

Our inspirations for this were the television programs *Little House on the Prairie* and *Grizzly Adams*. One afternoon we decided to finally do it as everyone, including my mother, had lied down for a nap. Katy and I snuck out the back door. We made it about four blocks before we realized that neither of us really knew how to get to the prairie. At this point we decided to go back home.

When we arrived, our mother was frantic. We knew we were in trouble, so we lied and told her we were kidnapped. She believed us and called the cops. The cops questioned us separately, resulting in Katy and me disagreeing on the alleged perpetrator's clothing.

After mockingly threatening to arrest us and giving us a lecture about the serious consequences of lying, the cops left our house laughing. After they left, however, my mother wasn't laughing. We both deservedly received the belt treatment.

Sixth grade marked a huge improvement for me academically, although I still made a few trips to the principal's office for school yard shenanigans. I finished that year with straight A's. This was the last time that I would make the honor roll.

When I entered junior high in the fall of 1985, I noticed how much taller and more muscular the other boys were than I. They had all hit their growth spurts in the summer while my own appeared to be stuck in neutral. The girls noticed this as well. I did not have a single date the entire two years.

I was a mediocre student, but I did enjoy learning. I loved science: especially astronomy and zoology; as well as history and English literature. My seventh-grade English teacher introduced me to Charles Dickens's *Great Expectations*. I read it cover to cover that winter. This became a holiday tradition for me for some time after that.

I enjoyed learning. My mind was a sponge, but I hated doing homework. I preferred, and still do prefer, to learn things informally; at my own leisure. My grades reflected this attitude.

CHAPTER III

A Change of Venue

IN THE FALL of 1987 I entered high school. I began the year at the Pekin Community High School's west campus. At that time, the junior varsity students attended classes here while the varsity students went to the east campus. About twenty years later, the school board elected to shut down the west campus and merge all the students at the east campus.

A week before classes started I spent some time at my father's house. While I was here, my mother gave birth to my little brother, Chad. Talk about a hairy baby! Chad was covered in hair from head to toe: on his head, shoulders, neck, back, etc. He looked just like a baby monkey. His hair was dark brown, and he had brown eyes to match.

My mother wanted me to cut my visit short, but I was having too much fun at my father's house. This hurt my mother's feelings, but at the time I only cared about myself.

In gym class, we spent two weeks studying the fundamentals and techniques of amateur wrestling, as well as the science behind it. At the beginning of the second week, our gym teacher told us we would have a competition at the end of the week to measure how much we'd learned.

We would be paired up by weight. At the time I only weighed ninety-eight pounds. The next closest student weighed one hundred thirty-six pounds and was the seventh- and eighth-grade state champion for his weight class.

All week long the other students taunted me in the gym, in the halls and even at lunch. The only student who remained silent was the kid I had to wrestle. He was mostly quiet all the time but somewhat friendly toward me.

The entire week I was a nervous wreck. I couldn't sleep or eat. I was basically shaking like a leaf up until the time of our match. The match was scheduled for three, one-minute rounds. Surprisingly, I did not get pinned. The match went the distance with me losing ten points to twelve.

After the match I was so exhausted and out of breath that I couldn't speak. Even if I had a breath left, speaking would have still been difficult as dry as my mouth was. All I could manage was a weak gesture toward the locker room at the coach.

He honored my request, and I staggered that direction like a drunken sailor on my rubbery legs. Upon returning to the gym about ten minutes later, the coach asked I to join the school's wrestling team. This was a request that both he and the student I wrestled would repeat, over and over again, for the next three weeks.

About this time the first semester was ending. I informed my mother that I wanted to go live with my father. Becky protested at first, but finally ceded as she did not wish to take the matter to court. At the time a boy had the legal right to decide for himself at the age of fourteen. I had been that age for a few months at this point.

I finished my first and only semester at the west campus, barely passing most of my classes. I did manage to get one *A* though, in world history. I was too preoccupied with sex and feelings of depression to apply myself adequately to the academics.

40

By this time my friend Brett had acquired a large collection of porn magazines and videos. My brother Michael had also been giving me an education on the subject.

Initially, Becky allowed me to take my dog Teddy with me to my father's house. Teddy was a collie with black and white markings. We called him Digity-Dog because of his outdoor habits.

I remember a few times when my father had come to pick me up after I was in bed. Teddy, who always slept at the foot of my bed, stood up and growled. He would not let Tony near me. Sadly, after two weeks, my mother changed her mind and took Teddy back home with her.

At the start of the second semester of my freshman year, I enrolled at Lewistown Community High School. The school was much smaller than the one in Pekin; with a student population of only three hundred fifty, compared to the five thousand at Pekin. Lewistown did not even have a wrestling program.

What Lewistown lacked in size, it more than made up for in character. In the classrooms the teachers were able to devote more time to each student. On the field everyone who tried out made the team. I joined the baseball team. I might not have played much, but at least I felt as if I were a part of something. It was also very nice that everyone knew each other on a first-name basis

That spring, Cheap Trick came out with a version of "Don't Be Cruel." I absolutely loved it. My stepmother Lisa told me that Elvis Presley sang it better. I did not believe her, so she got out the LP.

Singing had always been a passion of mine. When I was only six years old I copied all the lyrics to Kenny Rogers's "Lucille" from an eight track. This was not an easy task considering the playback mechanics of an eight-track player.

Kenny Rogers, Lionel Ritchie, Bryan Adams, Michael Jackson, and Rod Stewart were big-time idols of mine. From the moment I heard his voice, I fell in love with Elvis Presley.

My adoration became an obsession. Lisa lived to regret turning me on to Elvis. I never was much of a dancer, but I could sing most songs. The ones that I couldn't, I sang anyway. By the time I graduated high school, my family had forgotten what peace and quiet was.

The summer after my freshman year, hot pink spandex shorts were popular. One evening during a visit at my mother's house, my stepfather Kenny was folding our laundry. He came across my spandex shorts and asked whose they were. I told him they were mine, and he said:

"Only sissies wear pink."

We ended up in a shouting match at first that quickly led to a shoving match. I assumed he was going to attempt to pin me to the ground again like last time, so I put him in a headlock. I would not let go until he stopped struggling. When I finally did release him, he was out of breath; but that was the end of our altercation.

Later that week, Katy's best friend spent the night. Kenny caught the girl and me in bed together. He and I had an impromptu discussion about sexually transmitted diseases and unwanted pregnancies.

As soon as I returned home I began dating my first real girlfriend. Her name was Sara, and she was two years younger than I. I was fifteen at the time. Sara was short but well-proportioned with wavy sandy blond hair and green eyes. Her mother Heather was the owner of an auto alignment shop. She would take us cruising all the time. Sadly, neither my father nor my mother gave me any driver training. Heather made up for this.

At Christmas time, Sara's family showered me with gifts. They also gave me money to buy my own family some nice things. My mother still has the large mirror that I got her, hanging on her living-room wall.

That winter I broke up with Sara. I desired a more intimate relationship, but at thirteen, Sara was too young. Although our relationship lasted less than six months, that would turn out to be the norm for me throughout my life. She would be my last serious girlfriend for several years.

The spring of my sophomore year I began entering Elvis impersonator contests. I had become good friends with a kid who played on my brother Thomas's baseball team. His name was Alex, and he was short with wavy reddish brown hair and hazel eyes. What Alex did not have in size, he more than made up for in instinct and natural athletic ability.

Like me, Alex idolized Elvis Presley, even more so at the time. He had also learned to play the guitar. I spent the night at his house all the time. We would take turns singing Elvis songs and playing Super Mario Bros on Nintendo.

Alex was a much-better dancer than I was. He also tried unsuccessfully to teach me a few basic guitar chords. Unfortunately, I was blessed with no rhythm and two left thumbs.

Alex entered a lot of these contests with me. We would train together and even had a couple of jumpsuits tailor-made for us. Years later, the practice paid off for Alex as he took the guitar playing and singing, an art form for him at that point, on tour. By this time, he had expanded his repertoire to include mostly contemporary favorites.

My brother Thomas was quite a bit taller than Alex or me. He was practically born with a baseball glove in his hand. He was the star of every team that he played on and popular wherever he went. In spite of this, Thomas was humble and very considerate. The perfect little brother, which only added to his popularity.

Years later, Thomas attended Illinois Central College where still to this day; he is the record holder in several offensive categories. He even broke Jim Thome's record for most career home runs by a student. Sadly, at the end of his sophomore year, Thomas had an accident sliding into third base that ended his baseball career.

During the summer following my sophomore year, my best friend Brett was arrested on charges of child molestation. Brett asked me to be a witness for him. Several years earlier, Brett, Katy, and I had played "doctor" with another girl.

Aware of this information, my stepmother Lisa contacted the prosecuting attorney and shared it with him. When I took the stand the prosecutor asked me about it. Out of fear of perjury charges I told the truth. Brett was found guilty and received a few years in prison. Brett and I have not spoken since.

I had a few other good friends in high school. Among them was a guy named Andrew. Andrew was a year younger than I and an inch or two taller. He had short brown hair and brown eyes. Andrew was a walking, talking sports almanac. I never once heard him answer a sports-related trivia question incorrectly.

Andrew was also extremely overweight. If one had a decent arm, one could literally throw Andrew out at first base—from medium left field. In instincts and knowledge, Andrew was unparalleled, though. He once observed that the first baseman's shoe was off the bag, so Andrew slid into the bag headfirst. He was safe on a routine grounder to the shortstop to the amazement of us all!

Andrew's father used to organize Whiffle Ball tournaments every summer. As the town's athletic director he also coordinated overnight basketball tournaments in the school gymnasium from time to time.

Andrew, Thomas and I loved to play Whiffle Ball. We would travel all over town. Everyone's house was named after a different major-league park. On many occasions, Thomas would hit the ball over a roof, which was potentially a home run, only to have Andrew come walking around the corner a few minutes later, waving his glove in the air, claiming he caught the ball. An argument always ensued, which often lasted for a half hour.

Andrew also had connections for us to receive alcohol. We would have a lot of parties, but I did not like the taste of beer. I wanted to fit in and keep up with everyone, so I pretended to drink my beers, when, in actuality, I took them to the bathroom and dumped them out.

In English class during my junior year, I became infatuated with a cheerleader named Kimberly Murphy. Kimberly was of average height, with a thin build and medium complexion. Her hair was long, wavy and brown. Kimberly had big brown eyes.

If Kimberly looked at me a certain way with her eyebrow arched, it felt as if she were looking right through me. In my eyes, Kimberly was the personification of an angel and could do no wrong. I once asked her for a dance, but she politely refused. I never went to another dance after that.

That spring, our drama teacher gave us an assignment to write a short story. We were then instructed to read these stories in front of the class. Drawing upon my feelings of depression and the current events surrounding Elvis Presley faking his death, I wrote about a man who actually does fake his own death.

A friend of Kimberly's named Jasmine listened to me read my story. Jasmine had long black hair and brown eyes. She was fair-complected with a thin build. Jasmine was vice president of the student council and a member of the anti-suicide committee. This group was led by our history teacher, Mrs. Jones.

In part due to the subject matter; but mostly due to my inability to keep my emotions in check as I narrated, Jasmine showed pity upon me. She befriended me and told Mrs. Jones about the situation. Mrs. Jones took me under her wing.

Mrs. Jones was in her late forties and very short. She had graying light brown hair and huge glasses. She was a strict matter-of-fact lady who was pro-government and U.S. military.

In August of 1990, Saddam Hussein invaded the city-state of Kuwait. There was a huge multinational military buildup in the region as a result. This was the beginning of my senior year.

I was now a government student of Mrs. Jones. I idolized my history teacher and took everything that she said as the gospel truth. I decided to join the military after high school. I wanted to become a Marine and go over to Kuwait and *save the day*.

I was a month shy of my seventeenth birthday, so I needed parental consent to enlist. My stepmother, Lisa, told me that she did not want me coming home in a body bag like her uncle did. Lisa said that she would agree to my joining the Air Force or Navy, but not to my joining the Army or Marines Corps.

With my stepmother's consent, I signed a four year enlistment with the United States Navy. This was a week before my birthday. After the initial paperwork was completed I was tested and, based upon the result, I was given a list of Naval jobs to choose from. Without knowing what the job entailed, I selected Hospital Corpsman.

When Lisa heard about this she threw a fit. She asked:

"Out of all the jobs to choose from, you have to pick the Marine Corps medic?"

Lisa asked this because Marine Corps medics are actually Naval Hospital Corpsmen. As it was, I needed Lisa's consent to enlist; but not to choose my position.

That entire year I kept my decision to join the Navy to myself. I was obsessed about the undeserved reputation that sailors are gay. After my tour of duty actually ended, not only was I proud to have served in the Navy, but I also felt I had made the best choice.

Early during my senior year I got in a shouting match in the cafeteria with a fellow senior named Lance Jensen. Lance was average height, with a medium build and complexion. He had sandy brown hair and hazel eyes. He was typically an easy going guy.

A couple of days after our altercation, his girlfriend broke up with him. Lance was sitting by himself quietly in the cafeteria, so I approached him. At this point we were only acquaintances, but I still wanted to cheer him up.

I started by apologizing for our fight. Before long we were laughing and joking. After this, Lance and I became inseparable the entire year.

Lance helped me to come out of my shell somewhat; and in doing so, he expanded my horizons musically, theatrically and sociably. I spent the night with him often, and we would go cruising in his Trans-Am all the time. The driver's side door was broken so Lance always entered and exited the vehicle *Dukes of Hazzard*-style.

Lance played football and organized a fan club for the basketball team. The fan club was named: LOOSE, which stood for

Lewistown Outrageously Obnoxious Sports Enthusiasts. LOOSE had only three members: Lance, our friend Jeremiah Williams and I.

Jeremiah was tall and very thin. He had dark brown hair, brown eyes, and a dark complexion. He had poor vision and as a result he wore glasses with thick Coke-bottle lenses. Jeremiah and I were on the baseball team together where we only got to play once or twice the entire season.

Adding insult to injury, when our baseball team made it to the state finals, Jeremiah and I were downgraded to managers to meet roster restrictions. This meant that we would have to remain in the dugout the entire tournament.

During the regular season we would always take the field during warm-ups. We were both upset and offended by this. We felt that all the practicing we did all year earned us the right to at least take the field before the game. Jeremiah verbally complained about this. After high school, Jeremiah joined the U.S. Army, where he beefed up and honorably served for twenty years.

As members of LOOSE, the three of us would paint our faces and wear bandanas. We would attend all the home games, where we were notorious for being rowdy fans. We used to do acrobats along with the cheerleaders. We ruled the school in our own minds.

That was predominately the extent of my social interaction throughout my senior year. I did not attend our junior prom and two months before our senior one, I still did not have a date. I wanted to go with Kimberly, but she just laughed and shrugged her shoulders at that idea.

At the last minute, a junior by the name of Susie agreed to go with me. Susie was from a strict Christian family. She was only allowed to go to the promenade and dinner.

Our school had rented out a twenty-four-hour sports and fitness center for our after-prom activities. After a quick dinner, I dropped Susie off at home I headed for the fitness center.

I spent the whole night bowling by myself, watching sadly as everyone else seemed to be having fun—everyone except for

Kimberly. She was sitting a few lanes down from me looking

dejected as her friends bowled. I wanted so much to go talk to her,

but I did not possess the self-confidence that was necessary to do so.

CHAPTER IV

Full-Speed Ahead

THE FINAL THREE months of high school I welcomed

Christian missionaries of several different denominations into my

father's home. My spiritual mind had a craving for knowledge. I

entertained Mormons, Jehovah's Witnesses, and Lutherans; to name a

few.

To Lisa, a non-practicing Roman Catholic, this was pure

nonsense. She told me I was just like my mother: bouncing from

church to church. At one point, I stopped eating pork because I read

that it was wrong in the Bible. Lisa chastised me for this as well.

I began going to a nondenominational church with some high

school friends and even went to some Bible studies. The church was

named Christian Community Fellowship and the Bible studies were

led by a man named Timothy Lee.

Timothy was a thirty-eight year old, married father of two. He was tall, wore glasses and had short, thinning brown hair. Timothy was a very humble man who encouraged us to think critically as we examined the texts.

After graduating high school with a *D* average, Katy and I flew down to Huntsville, Alabama, to see our paternal grandmother. We had never flown before so we argued all the way to the airport about which of us was going to sit next to the window.

The first leg of our journey we boarded a small commuter plane destined for Nashville, Tennessee. Although we were the only two passengers on the flight, we still argued. A stewardess approached us and suggested that we both sit by a window, as there were obviously plenty of empty seats to go around. It was a *genius* idea, and so that is precisely what we did.

To this day, I love to fly. I get really nervous before the plane departs. I consider the possibility that I could be dead in a few minutes. I also pray in an attempt to get all my affairs in order. I find the takeoff particularly exhilarating, as I don't know if I'll live or die.

Once we have reached our cruising altitude, the adrenaline rush is replaced by a somber feeling that is highlighted by wonder. As I look down at the ground far below, everything looks so peaceful and perfect. To me, it looks exactly like the landscape of a model train set: No potholes in the streets, all the grass is perfectly green and the fields are perfect geometric shapes.

When we landed in Huntsville, our grandparents were at the airport to meet us. Grandma Stephenson was a short lady with brown hair and eyes. She had a thin build and a soft heart. Grandpa Stephenson was a tall man with broad shoulders. He had short white hair, and he worked for NASA.

Katy and I spent a week with them. While we were there, Grandma Stephenson took us out to eat, to a water park and to an observatory high up in the mountains. Before we left, we even got a brief tour of NASA.

During the afternoons, Katy would sunbathe in the backyard. She would always get a nice dark brown tan. Try as I might, I could never understand why I was only able to get a burn.

The night before our visit ended, Grandma Stephenson gave each of us twenty dollars and took us to the mall. I used my money to by paperback Bibles at the dollar store. My intention was to pass them out to people after I returned home.

When I arrived, Lisa was irate. She told me I had to return the Bibles and get my money back. I told her I was a grown man now; and that she could no longer tell me what to do or how to spend my money. Lisa responded by informing me that I was no longer welcome in her home.

With less than a month to go before I shipped off for boot camp I moved back in with my mother. Becky was overjoyed to have me back.

Every morning around four A.M., I got dressed and ran to the mall three miles away. I would rest for fifteen minutes; and then turn around and run back. I was famous for my running speed, but my body was conditioned for shorter distances. As a result, this was a very painful endeavor at first.

Eventually I was able to complete the task with minimal discomfort. At this point, I was confident that I was physically ready for the military. Katy used to get up early, as well, and join me on my runs. She would always fall behind me. I used to shout at her over my shoulder:

"You better kick it in the butt, if you are going to keep up with me!"

On July 15, 1991, I took a bus to the Military Enlisted Processing Station (MEPS) in Des Plaines, Illinois. Once there, we had dinner before we were subjected to written and physical examinations. After this, we were lodged up in a dorm-style setting for the night. Bright and early the following morning, a *chariot* arrived to transport us to "hell".

When we arrived at Great Lakes Recruit Training Command, we were all initially nervous about what we had just gotten ourselves into. We were greeted by a Latino who could not have been much more than four feet tall. He began screaming at us in military jargon that few, if any, of us, understood.

We all let out a sigh of relief as we thought this is not going to be so bad after all. We mocked the man as he continued to scream at us, as we defiantly *marched* to chow—which stands for meal-time in military terminology. After chow, we went through a briefing that lasted what seemed like hours.

Next we were officially swore in and ordered to turn in our civilian clothes, as well as everything else that connected us to the outside world. After this; we received a set of uniforms, a set of personal hygiene items and a white mesh ditty bag to carry them all in.

We were also issued a sea bag to stow all of our military uniforms in. A sea bag is a forest green burlap sack that is fitted with shoulder straps. Soldiers and sailors alike can be observed carrying sea bags on their backs as they march.

Afterward, the short man lined us up and marched us to the processing barracks, shouting all the way. We were talking and laughing the entire time.

The next morning, very early, we were abruptly awakened by the sound of a metal trash can bouncing the entire length of the concrete barracks floor. This ruckus was accompanied by an angry and very loud voice demanding that we get out of our racks and stand in front of them. I hardly knew what a rack was at this point— especially this early in the morning. However, because the voice was so frightening, I mimicked the other recruits and followed them to the front of our racks.

As we stood there bewildered in our skivvies (underwear), we glanced in unison down toward the end of the room. We were determined to size up the man behind that terrible voice. This was a huge mistake!

The man behind the voice was our company commander. A company commander is the Naval equivalent for drill sergeant. This man was a dark-skinned African American, who stood about six-foot-seven inches tall and was about three hundred pounds of muscle.

To make our situation worse, he was furious. We were not to look directly at him. He informed us of this in a loud voice which was generously punctuated with un-Christian-like verbiage.

At one point he got in a recruit's face. This scared the young man to the point that he literally urinated on himself. I was down at the other end of the barracks, but I could distinctly hear it as it hit the concrete floor. Looking back, it was quite hilarious but no one dared laugh at the time.

Chief Turnip was his name, and if we thought about laughing, we quickly changed our minds; as he immediately made us drop to the deck (floor) and do push-ups for our shipmate's lack of self-control. We quickly learned that if one of us messes up, for the most part, we all get punished. We also found out that we would not be taught our military terminology in a kind and considerate fashion.

Chief Turnip eventually called us to our feet and ordered us get dressed. To an outside observer it would have been quite comical to watch us desperately trying to put on our uniforms for the very first time.

He then set us up in formation and silently marched us to chow. *We* were silent, that is. Chief Turnip continued to bark foreign instructions to us all the way there.

Once we arrived, we stood heel to toe in formation and remained silent. We stood this way in front of the chow hall for about thirty minutes. Once we were given permission to march inside, we had to stop and wait for another fifteen minutes before we could sit down and eat.

Eventually, it was our turn to eat. We were given fifteen minutes to do so. We learned that talking in formation or while we were eating was forbidden. (Although this silence was only observed during basic training.) We also learned that we did everything as a unit. Our individuality disappeared the moment we took the oath.

The next eight-and-a-half weeks of our existence became a routine. Chief Turnip would tell us he was going to wake us up at five, but would most often wake us up at three. Our days consisted of:

- Reveille (Wake up call accompanied by a trumpet)

- Physical training

- Chow

- Drills

- More physical training

- Chow

- Naval classes

- Still more physical training

- Chow

- More Naval classes

- Personal time

- Tattoo (five minute warning to prepare for bed)

- Taps (bedtime)

I was assigned the ceremonial title of Religious Petty Officer of my company. Each of us was issued a pocket sized New Testament, which also included the Books of Psalms and Proverbs. Each night before the lights went out; I would read my shipmates a Scripture or two and then lead them in a prayer.

We were all so physically exhausted, due to a lack of sleep, that we would actually fall asleep standing in lines. Luckily, the feeling of our relaxing bodies collapsing would normally awaken us, before we injured ourselves.

In the classrooms, where we were able to sit down, sailors were constantly nodded off. Each time, they would be abruptly awakened by an angry shipmate or two. This repeatedly demonstrated hostility could be directly attributed to our fear of a group reprimand by the instructors. As we were dropped as a unit on many occasions for various discrepancies.

Periodically, we were subjected to uniform and living quarter's inspections. One day we had an indoor uniform inspection. It was protocol when an officer entered a room for the first person that saw him to announce:

"Attention on deck!"

When the alarm was sounded, we quickly got into formation and stood at attention. Chief Turnip shouted,

"Where are your @%* covers?"

A *cover* is military terminology for hat. No one answered him except for me. Those years of keeping my mouth shut around David Gillespie had finally taken its toll on me.

The man asked a question, so I responded:

"We are not authorized to wear our covers indoors, so we assumed they were not required for this inspection, sir."

Military formations are set up tallest to shortest. The racks of the tallest recruits are at the front of the barracks; those of the shortest recruits' are near the back of the room. There were only two recruits shorter than me.

Without saying a word, Chief Turnip slowly marched back to me. He deliberately emphasized his approach with each step that he made. He got in my face and screamed in my ear about how arrogant

I was. He then made an exception to the rule of uniformity, by making me drop and do push-ups, solo, while he inspected the rest of his troops.

Throughout basic training, we had mail call each evening just before tattoo. I only received two letters the entire time. Both of which came from my mother.

I wrote letters as often as I could; including two or three to Kimberly. We had a bulletin board at the entrance to the berthing area. We were allowed to post photographs here. I posted a picture of her.

The day before we graduated from boot camp, I turned eighteen years old. This day was also referred to as "Family Day". Not in my honor, of course! The families of recruits were allowed to come on the base and spend the entire day with them. The recruit and his family were also allowed to leave the base for a few hours.

The recruits who did not have any family members present were required to stay on the base and work. On my eighteenth birthday, I worked.

The final night of basic training, Chief Turnip allowed us to relax and sit in a semicircle on the deck. He then pulled up a chair and sat in front of us. Chief Turnip critiqued each of us one by one. He told me:

"You are arrogant, Smith. I see many bumps in the road ahead for you. Eventually you will be successful though, because you are not afraid to speak your mind."

The next morning we said our good-byes to Chief Turnip and Recruit Training Command.

Every month in the U.S. military, a service member receives two-and-a-half days of leave per month. A *leave* is the military equivalent of a paid vacation. This equates to thirty vacation days a year. This is the same rate regardless of your rank; or whether you are enlisted or commissioned.

Unused leave time could be accumulated up to a period of four years. On the other hand, leave time could be used in advance, provided that special permission was granted. I found the military to be quite agreeably liberal in honoring those requests. Upon my completion of basic training, I requested to take my first two weeks right away. My request was immediately granted. .

I flew home and met with my mother's side of the family. My mother, Becky showed me a couple of photographs she had taken of my brother Chad. Chad was four at this point. The photographs were a before-and-after depiction of him sitting in a barber's chair. In the first one, Chad's hair was long. In the second one, he had a crew cut. On the back Becky wrote,

"Wouldn't you say that he looks ready for the Navy now?"

We didn't really have much to talk about beyond that; so after a day or two, I went to my father's house.

As I arrived everyone seemed genuinely happy to see me. Lisa made a really nice dinner for me and we talked for hours that first night. My brother Thomas introduced me to his new girlfriend Sandy Duncan.

Sandy had just begun her senior year at Lewistown. I didn't really know Sandy, but I knew of her. She was a short, blond-haired, green-eyed girl with a nicely proportioned physique. She was a stunningly beautiful young lady. Years later, Thomas and Sandy would tie the knot. Unfortunately, I was unable to attend their wedding ceremony.

My brother Michael informed me that he was considering joining the Army. I told him he should join the Navy instead. Michael just laughed at me.

After this, I made an appearance at my old high school. I proudly showed up in uniform. Eight weeks of Naval training had eliminated my reservations, in regards to the stereotypes of that particular service.

I received a special pass to sit in on Mrs. Jones' government class. She was very happy to see me and proud of how far I had come in the past eighteen months. I graciously thanked her, and told her that she had a lot to do with it. I told Mrs. Jones that she had been a huge inspiration to me.

She asked me to speak to her class. I spoke to them about patriotism and the importance of the U.S. military. I also stressed to them about how lonely servicemen can become away from home, and how important letters are to them.

After leaving the high school I immediately tracked down my old friend Lance. Our buddy Jeremiah was not able to be there, because he had already left for Army training. For the first time in my life I actually drank a beer and liked it. Lance and I proceeded to party together for an entire week. This was the first time that I had ever been intoxicated.

Sadly, my leave time ended too soon. My orders—military paperwork pertaining to duty station assignment, instructed me to report to Hospital Corpsman School, which was also located at Great Lakes. We often referred to it as:

"Great Mistakes"

and to the Navy in general as:

 N-ever

A-gain

V-olunteer

Y-ourself.

After reluctantly reporting for duty, I quickly discovered; to my grateful surprise, that this was not the Navy that I had been accustomed to over the past three months. There were no more forced push-ups. There was no more screaming, a lot more respect and a ton of free time!

We were now required to be in class every morning at six A.M. and still had to march to chow together. We were also expected to keep our rooms orderly and our bodies and uniforms up to military specifications (specs).

The rest of the time we could do whatever we chose—including leaving the base. We now had about an hour to eat, and we were allowed to sit where we wanted and talk as much as we wished.

The classes lasted about three-and-a-half months. During this time we learned:

- Anatomy & Physiology

- First aid and cardiopulmonary resuscitation (CPR) protocol

- Heat stroke, hypothermia and shock prevention assessment and treatment

- Immunization administration

- Catheterization and intravenous injections (IV's) administration

- Cast & splint administration

- Pharmaceuticals

- Medication administration

Our education was basically a crash course of what was required of a licensed vocational or practical nurse (LVN/LPN).

For the most part, I applied myself to my studies. I went out quite a bit, but I refrained from drinking. I made an exception to my disciplined lifestyle over Thanksgiving weekend.

Our school was shut down for the holiday. Since my hometown was only a couple of hours away, I decided to fly home for the weekend. I wore my uniform on the flight and proudly ordered a beer. Out of respect for my uniform, the stewardess served me without question. I was a very happy eighteen-year-old.

My flight was redirected to a city a few miles from the plane's intended destination. I called my father for a ride home. When Tony arrived to pick me up, he could not find me at first. He eventually located me after following a trail of vomit to the ladies' room. Tony discovered me there, passed out in one of the stalls.

The next afternoon I enjoyed a pleasant Thanksgiving dinner with my father's side of the family. Afterward, I tracked down my buddy Lance. The two of us drank heavily the remainder of the weekend. I did not visit my mother's side of the family at all.

I returned to school hung-over, early the following Monday morning. Luckily, I was able to focus and apply myself enough to finish the final two months of training.

On January 30, 1992, I graduated from Naval Hospital Corpsman School; second in my class of eighty with a ninety-six percent. The top five percent had the option of taking an advanced training of their choice. I chose Neuropsychiatric Technician School. Classes did not convene for another couple of months, so I took another two-week leave.

Tony and Thomas came to my graduation. It was as much touching to me as it was unexpected to see my father there. Afterward, I rode home with them. I did not drink the entire time I was home. I also took some time to visit with my mother, Terry, Katy, Brooke and little Chad.

CHAPTER V

A Crazy Thing Called Psychiatric Medicine

AFTER RETURNING TO my command I still had about a month before my psychiatric technician classes convened. While awaiting the school to start I was assigned to the records department at Naval Hospital Great Lakes. I was in charge of filing and retrieving outpatient records. It was important for me to accurately validate that the individuals who were requesting the records, were authorized to receive them.

There were only four of us who worked in the health records department. The other three were permanently assigned there.

The Leading Petty Officer (LPO) was Jesus Martinez. Jesus was a short, stocky Mexican American with black hair and brown eyes. He was in his mid-thirties. He was a quiet man who rarely cracked a smile and as LPO, he was in charge of our group.

Mike Austin, Andre Lucas and I rounded out the group. Mike was a short, chubby Caucasian who was barely able to avoid being medically discharged for violating the Navy's strict no-body-fat policy. Mike was twenty-seven years old; he had blue eyes and dyed his hair blond.

Andre was a tall, athletically built African American with green eyes. He was twenty-four years old. Altogether, we made for quite an interesting group of individuals.

Mike and Andre shared an apartment off base. I lived in a dorm on base. I shared my living quarters with two others.

At work, our shifts were Monday through Friday; six A.M. to five P.M. The very first Friday afternoon, just prior to the end of our work day, Mike invited me to a party at his apartment. As I was too young to purchase alcohol for myself, I enthusiastically accepted his invitation.

Up until this point, I had only drunken beer and a sip of a wine cooler my mother gave me years earlier. That all changed at Mike's party. Vodka, peach schnapps, beer and wine were all freely available. I tried everything; favoring the schnapps and wine. A group of high school girls joined us, and we partied all weekend.

One girl was tall, fair-skinned, and named Tara. Tara had green eyes and short hair, which she dyed orange.

Tara's best friend was a short, medium-built Jewish girl named Cindy Ruth. Cindy had big brown eyes and shoulder-length brown hair. She used a plastic headband to keep her bangs out of her eyes. Tara and Cindy were both fifteen.

The first night that I met them was a Saturday evening. I had been drinking Boone's Farm wine straight from the liter bottle since the night before. Not long after we were introduced, I passed out on the floor in the corner of the apartment and began to vomit.

Cindy became worried that I might aspirate. She walked over and sat down beside me. She lifted my head off the floor and rested it in her lap.

I thanked Cindy for her passionate generosity by vomiting on her repeatedly. In spite of this, Cindy and Tara partied with us every weekend after that until my classes began.

In early March of 1992, I departed Great Lakes for the didactic (classroom) portion of my psychiatric technician school. This school was located at an Army base, named Fort Sam Houston. This base was situated on the outskirts of San Antonio, Texas.

After saying my goodbyes and departing from Illinois, I kept in contact with both Cindy and Tara for a while. After some time, I lost contact with Tara. Over the years, Cindy would continue to be a friend, whose path would cross mine a number of times.

The first thing that I did when I arrived at Ft. Sam Houston was check in at the dorm where I would be staying. I also met my two roommates, Tim and Marvin.

Tim was a twenty-six-year-old, tall Caucasian with brown hair and eyes. Marvin was a nineteen-year-old Mexican American of average height, with a medium-to-athletic build. They were both in the Navy and had identical orders to my own.

After stowing my gear, I staggered down to the chow hall. In military terminology staggering means to walk out of formation; solo or in small groups. Upon entering and observing where the chow line began, I was approached by a man dressed in army fatigues.

He told me the first thing I needed to do was go back to the barracks and get in uniform. (I was dressed in blue jeans at the time.) He said the second thing I needed to do was go get a haircut. I told him:

"I'm Navy, sir."

He replied:

"The first thing you need to do is address me as First Sergeant as I am noncommissioned. The second thing you need to do since, you are one of those Navy 'homosexuals', is get in line over there quick; if you want something to eat!"

He then smirked at me and walked away chuckling.

Our classes were Monday through Friday. My fellow students were equally represented by both Naval and Army personnel. My Army classmates had to live in a barracks. They were required to march everywhere they went and they were not permitted to leave the base.

For the Navy students, life at Ft. Sam Houston was even more relaxed than Hospital Corpsman School. We were only required to be on time for class every morning—clean shaven and in uniform. We had a lot of free time and we were allowed to leave the base as often as we desired.

In the Navy, we were allowed to grow our hair longer than our Army comrades could. I had a habit of bringing hairspray to class with me each morning. I would enter the latrine (Army term for restroom) before class started and fix my hair.

Late one evening while I was enjoying a drink with Tim and Marvin at a local cantina, I was approached by a man who I didn't know. He was shorter than I and sported a crew cut.

He asked me if I was the pretty boy who brought hairspray to class with him every morning. I stood up; but before I could respond verbally, this little man had me by my throat and off my feet. As my feet dangled above the ground, he slammed me against a wall and held me there. He said:

"I'm a Navy SEAL. You are giving the Navy a bad image. Don't ever 'freaking' do that again."

He then released his grip and let me fall to the ground. No sooner had I hit the deck, when he reached down with one hand and yanked me to my feet. His stern look was quickly replaced by a toothy grin as he laughed heartily. His laugh filled up the entire room.

He then put his arm over my shoulder and said to his friends:

"Now let's teach this baby how a *real* sailor drinks."

The SEAL then ordered a round of tequila and pushed a glass in front of me. This went on relentlessly for over three hours. I did not like the taste of the tequila, but I drank it anyway.

Tim and Marvin had to literally carry me to the car afterwards. The next morning, I was late for class and given non-judicial punishment. This amounted to sixteen hours of community service, where I was assigned extra-duty, washing dishes in the chow hall.

Besides returning to the cantina on a regular basis, we toured San Antonio quite a bit. San Antonio, Texas, with its beautiful women and friendly citizens; became one of the favorite places in the world that I had ever visited.

There is a tower in San Antonio that you can tour. The observation deck at the top is surrounded by a concrete wall about four feet high. This wall is topped off by an iron spiked fence that extends upward and outwards, by eight or nine feet, at a forty-five degree angle.

I have always had a fear of heights. I have even had reoccurring nightmares where I am either falling down some stairs or falling perpetually in mid-air. On this occasion, I decided to face my fears. I stood up on the top of the wall and stuck my face through the gap between two of the iron bars. The adrenaline rush that I got was beyond description. Although I encouraged them, Tim and Marvin refused to join me atop the wall.

The next day I received a letter from Katy. She told me she was pregnant and about to get married to her high school sweetheart, John. John and Katy were only two years younger than I was. I had known him for some time.

John was well over six feet tall. He had brown hair, green eyes and a muscular physique. He had been dating Katy since they were only thirteen years old. I had already considered him my brother and I was happy to hear about the marriage and pregnancy, but I was concerned because they were still in high school.

My fears were realized a few days later when Katy told me she had decided to drop out of school and get her GED. She reasoned that this way, she could get a job to save up some money for Nicole. Katy had already picked out a name for the baby before she knew if it was going to be a boy or a girl!

At the center of downtown San Antonio is a four-mile long, man-made canal that is surrounded on both sides by a hotel and a four-story megamall. This area is known collectively as the *San Antonio River Walk*. The hotel was an architectural marvel for its time. The hotel was designed to look two-dimensional from the perspective of the canal. The canal offered cheap gondola rides every night; and as you approached the hotel, it looked as if it was about to fall over.

The ground level of the mall was densely populated by restaurants and bars. Each one boasted outdoor patio seating. As you ate your meal or enjoyed a cocktail, a trio of Mexican men wearing large sombreros and dressed in flashy tuxedos would approach you, strumming their guitars. For a couple of dollars they would play you a love song.

I've always been a romantic at heart. I enjoy love songs, candlelight dinners, and sappy movies. Their performances deeply enhanced my experience in San Antonio.

Marvin was born and raised in Houston, Texas, but he also had family in Mexico. One Friday afternoon, he decided to go down to Mexico for the weekend. Unfortunately, Marvin accidentally left his military identification in our room.

When he attempted to cross the border back into the United States, Marvin was stopped and detained by the border patrol. My unfortunate shipmate remained in custody for well over a day, before the military went down to the Mexican border and retrieved him.

The very next weekend, Tim rented a car and said he would like us to join him on a road trip down the Gulf Coast. We accepted his invitation, packed our bags and headed out. Within three hours, San Antonio and Corpus Christi were behind us and we approached the beaches of South Padre Island.

As we arrived at the beach, we noticed that we were alone. Spring Break was still a few weeks away. Tim produced a liter of Crown Royal, and we proceeded to drink and play in the water. That night marked a couple of firsts for me.

It was the first time I had ever drank whiskey, and it was also the first time that I had ever experienced saltwater, firsthand. At dusk, Marvin built a campfire for us and we continued to party into the wee hours of morning.

The next morning we packed up our gear and headed for Mexico. We made sure that Marvin had his identification with him this time. I had never been out of the country before, so I was really excited.

When we arrived in Mexico, we parked Tim's car, rented a cheap room for the night and went to dinner. When our server asked us what type of libation we would prefer, I asked her what the special was. She told me margaritas.

Unaware that margaritas were made with tequila, I ordered one. When our drinks arrived I took one sip of mine and immediately felt sick. I ran to the restroom and made it just in time before I actually did get sick. Tim and Marvin thought this was very funny.

After dinner, we hit the bars. The only thing I could stomach was beer. Every time I tried to drink liquor I got sick, to the continued enjoyment of my shipmates.

After a night of heavy partying and very little rest, we rode non-stop back to base the next morning. I felt sick all day. Luckily for me, it was Sunday. I had an entire day to recuperate.

Six weeks after I arrived, my classes were complete. It was time for me to say good-bye to San Antonio; as well as my friends, Tim and Marvin. I truly had an unforgettable time in San Antonio. I've always said that I would return to San Antonio someday. Sadly, that day has not happened yet.

The final phase of our psychiatric technician training was our clinical (on-the-job- training). We each had orders to different locations. My orders were to San Diego, California.

The first week of May 1992, I flew to San Diego. I enjoyed myself so much in San Antonio that I was not looking forward to San Diego. My orders were to report to Naval Hospital Balboa. Balboa was within walking distance of downtown and the San Diego Zoo.

During that era, Naval Hospital Balboa was among the most technologically advanced in the entire military. Balboa boasted state-of-the-art equipment, including robots that took meals to the patients' rooms.

After reporting for duty, I was informed that the dorms were full so I would have to live in the barracks. This was the first time since boot camp that I had to share the head with around eighty other men. I missed San Antonio immediately.

In San Diego, you were allowed to drink on base if you were at least eighteen. There were a couple of clubs that I frequented on a regular basis. One night at the club, I met an African American named Tom.

Tom was an x-ray technician permanently assigned to Balboa. He was tall and had a medium build and complexion. As he was a full-time staff member, Tom lived in the dorm. After a couple rounds of shots, Tom invited me back to his room. Tom told me he normally drinks with his roommate, but he was currently on leave.

I joined Tom in his room, and not long thereafter, I experienced my first blackout. (The earlier time at the airport I had passed out, not blacked out.) I came to several hours later sprawled out on his bathroom floor surrounded by a mess.

Apparently during my blackout, I had lost control of my bodily functions. This would mark the beginning of a lifetime of blackouts and shameful actions during them for me.

I spent nearly every weekend of my time in San Diego across the border in Tijuana, Mexico. I always traveled with a couple of friends. The first time I went down there I noticed how different the world looked from one side of the fence to the other.

On the Tijuana side of the border, poverty hit me like a ton of bricks. I saw five-year-olds peddling oranges and cigarettes. I saw twelve-year-olds prostituting themselves on nearly every corner. It was very sad.

After the sun went down, we hit the clubs. I blacked out almost every time trip. It was not until our fifth trip, that I actually remembered going home. On that trip, I argued with my shipmates as we walked back. I told them that we were going the wrong way. They insisted that I was incorrect and finally won our argument, by informing me that they had to carry me back all the other times.

Three weeks before graduation, my commanding officer received a message that my grandfather had passed away. He was actually my stepmother Lisa's father. However, I had known him my whole life, and he treated me like one of his own. Grandpa Charlie was a tall man with a big nose. An accident caused him to lose two of his fingers on his right hand. He had white hair and blue eyes.

Grandpa Charlie was stern but fair. I requested, and was promptly granted emergency leave for his funeral.

Michael had joined the Army by this juncture. He also arrived home on emergency leave. We went to the funeral in uniform; Michael in his dress greens and me in my dress whites. Afterward, we went to Grandpa Charlie's house and had dinner with his widow, Grandma Lois.

Grandma Lois was a short redhead with green eyes. She was also a devote Roman Catholic. After spending the night at her house, I had to return to San Diego.

Upon my return, I found myself homesick and very depressed. The death of my grandfather weighed heavily upon me. My drinking increased, my uniform began to look ragged and even my participation in class began to wane.

At one point, my instructor considered removing me from the school entirely. He gave me an ultimatum: I either got it together, or I was gone. Ultimately, I graduated with the rest of my class.

One year after I went to boot camp, my training was finally complete. I received my orders and was assigned to Oak Knoll Naval Hospital in Oakland, California. This would be my first and only permanent duty station.

CHAPTER VI

The Boys of Skid Row

ON JUNE 26, 1992, I arrived in Oakland, California. After checking into the dorm and stowing my gear, I reported to my commanding officer. He instructed me to report to ward 5-north, the inpatient psychiatric unit.

Upon arrival, I met my LPO, HM2 Rollins. HM2 Rollins was a twenty-eight-year-old Scottish American with red hair and a round face. He had a ruddy complexion to add to his reflective demeanor.

HM2 Rollins introduced me to HN Barry Mount. Barry had been on staff at Oak Knoll for about a month. Barry was tall and had a large build. He had black hair, brown eyes, and a dark complexion. HM2 Rollins instructed Barry to orientate me to the ward.

Barry showed me where the nursing station was and introduced me to the current patients and the rest of the staff members. He then showed me all of the rooms, which included: the treatment room, the various intake interview rooms and the recreational room.

After this, Barry introduced me to HA Jeff Simpson. Barry and Jeff had been through every step of their training together. Jeff took a two-week leave prior to arriving at Oak Knoll, so Barry had seniority.

Jeff was about an inch taller than I, and he had a thin build. He had light brown hair, hazel eyes and a light complexion. Barry and Jeff shared a room at the dorm.

Working on the psych ward was about as easy a job as someone in the military could ask for. We had five, eight-hour shifts a week. There were three shifts a day, seven days a week.

Our schedules rotated every two months. Occasionally, we had to work weekends or the graveyard shift. The graveyard shift was hands-down, the best. Our responsibilities on this shift were to check on the patients once an hour, fill out nursing notes at the end of the shift, and do an intake interview and draw the blood of any patients that we received throughout the night.

We rarely received patients during those hours and of the capacity eighteen that we did have, seventy percent of them were not even mentally ill. Most of our patients were military personnel who were *acting* in the hopes of receiving a medical discharge. We spent most of the night playing spades, All Madden '92 on Sega and watching television.

On a psych ward, it is important to keep at least four staff members on duty at all times. This is in the unfortunate circumstance that a patient needs to be restrained. On those occasions, one staff member would be assigned per limb.

On our ward, we only had three techs assigned on the graveyard shift. Once a month we would be assigned a watch. This watch consisted of sleeping on a cot in the office next door. We would be on call to assist in a restraint situation.

The rest of our time we were free to come and go as we pleased. Barry, Jeff and I quickly formed a close bond. For much of our time in Oakland, we were inseparable. Depending on whom you talked to, we were often referred to as the *Three Musketeers* or *Skid Row.*

The three of us spent much of our time taking the BART (Bay Area Transit System) to the surrounding areas, including underground to San Francisco across the Bay. On one of these trips we stopped to get something to eat. When our waitress arrived and offered us something to drink I asked:

"What kind of alcohol do you have?"

The waitress knew right away that I was not twenty-one. I ended up drinking a glass of coke, after my wise server suggested it..

A few days later, we went to the Haight-Ashbury District of San Francisco. At the time, that district was the focal point of the city's drug and music scene. We checked out some of the used record stores where I found and purchased a set of Elvis cassettes.

Afterward, Jeff purchased a bag of marijuana from a man off the street. After returning to our dorm later that night, Jeff packed a pipe and offered Barry and me a hit. Barry accepted right away. I hesitated at first. I had never taken one puff of a cigarette in my entire life and considered the prospect disgusting.

After a little encouragement and a couple of drinks, I gave it a shot. I immediately felt light-headed and sick to my stomach. These feelings were only momentary. I soon noticed my tongue starting to feel numb and my voice beginning to sound like one of *David Seville's chipmunks*. Even these feelings didn't last long. I quickly become drowsy and went back to my room to sleep.

A few weeks later we returned to Haight-Ashbury. Jeff once again picked up some more weed; in addition, he purchased a half dozen hits of acid. On the tram ride back to the base, Jeff and Barry each took a hit. Jeff offered me one, but I declined. I had never had acid before, so I was concerned about how it would affect my body; particularly in public. After we returned to their room, I tried it.

Within seconds, my mouth seemed to come alive. Within ten minutes, the rest of my body followed suit. I could feel the rhythm of every inch of my body. It seemed as if I could literally feel my pupils inhaling and exhaling. I enjoyed that sensation.

We spent the entire night laughing and attempting to have philosophical conversations. We ended up starting a sentence, losing our train of thought, and repeating ourselves. We never got to the point.

We listened to the first two lines of *Golden Earring's "When the Bullet Hits the Bone"* for six hours straight. I tripped for a solid twelve hours on one hit.

Over the next year and a half; Jeff, Barry and I would make many more trips to Haight-Ashbury. On rare occasions, Jeff would score some acid for us, but mostly, he just bought weed. I would beg him to buy acid, but he usually ignored me. Once he said to me:

"If you want acid, get it yourself."

We would always combine our funds for the purchases, and Jeff would complete the transaction. I was nervous about getting arrested so I never stepped up to Jeff's challenge of buying my own acid.

I rarely smoked weed with him after that first time. My reason was a combination of my not really enjoying it and being paranoid that I would fail a military urine exam. Once a month the base commander selected a number between zero and nine. If the last number of your Social Security Number was the number that he selected, you had to give a urine sample. If you tested positive for drugs; you were restricted to the base for forty-five days, and then given a dishonorable discharge. Sadly, a month after I got out of the Navy, Jeff's number was drawn. He failed.

On our base we had a retail store that was known as a *Navy Exchange*. I applied for a credit account with them and was approved for eleven hundred dollars. I immediately went on a shopping spree. I purchased a television set, a stereo system, a huge microwave, and a karaoke machine with several cassettes.

That fall I recorded a Christmas album. I was serious about the album and as a result, several of the songs required more than thirty takes before I was satisfied. Many of these sessions went on until the early-morning hours. I did my recordings in my room while my roommates were at work. Surprisingly, I never received any feedback from my neighbors—positive or negative.

In its final form, the album consisted of twelve songs on the forty-five minute *A* side, and outtakes from the studio sessions on the *B* side. I was ultimately proud of my work. I made about twenty copies and sent them to my family and friends back home. Not one of my family members made any comment about the tape.

I also sent a copy to my friend Cindy. She loved it. After losing contact with her for some time, Cindy was still talking about that tape over twenty years later.

On November 26, 1992, Katy gave birth to her first child; a little girl that she named Nicole. I was overjoyed as I was an uncle for the very first time! I would not meet Nicole until after her first birthday, but that didn't matter. I was so happy for Katy and John.

The following January, our fleet was planning a trip to the Middle East. While the ships were stationed stateside, there was not a high demand for a large onboard medical department. For the most serious situations, the sailors could be med-evacuated to Oak Knoll. Of course, this was not practical if that sailor was halfway around the world, so before the fleet departed on a West Pac (Western Pacific) Tours, our commanding officer would ask for volunteers to go one the journey with them.

At the very last minute I volunteered. To be approved I had to submit a request chit that required the signature of five individuals. The first signature had to come from HM2 Rollins. I then had to acquire the signatures of my division officer, the command master chief, the executive officer, and finally my commanding officer.

This was commonly referred to as going up your chain of command. I was promptly approved at every level, quickly packed my sea bag, and made it to the dock just as they were pulling up the anchor. After eighteen months in the Navy, I was about to be underway for the very first time!

CHAPTER VII

Anchors Aweigh

MY ORDERS WERE to the USS *Kansas City (AOR-3)*. At first glance, the ship appeared to be huge. The *Kansas City* was the supply ship for the fleet. Besides food, equipment, and other essentials; our ship also refueled the other vessels underway. This earned the *Kansas City* as well as the other ships in its class (AOR) the nickname, the:

"Gas station of the Navy."

Once aboard, I was promptly escorted to the medical department. Here, I met the shipmates who I would be working closely with for the next six months.

First I met HM3 Stokley. He had reddish brown hair and hazel eyes, a fair complexion, and a thin build. HM3 Stokley was the x-ray technician of our group.

Next, I met HN Miller, our lab technician. HN Miller was a freckle-faced redhead with green eyes. He had a ruddy complexion and a large build.

HM2 Smith specialized in first aid and emergency room procedures. He acquired these skills after serving six years with the Second Marine Division. HM2 Smith was a tall, muscular African American who had a dark complexion. He was also an amateur boxer.

Our division officer was Lt. Thompson. He was a tall, thin Chinese American with thick Coke-bottle glasses. HM1 Reyes, our LPO, rounded out the group of sailors who were permanently assigned to the *Kansas City*. HM1 Reyes was a chubby Filipino American of average height. Unlike the rest of us, he did not begin his Naval career as a corpsman. He first spent a decade as a boatswain's mate. This job required him to work with the lines and equipment on the top deck.

Besides myself, there were two other sailors temporarily assigned to the *Kansas City*, a navy dentist, LCMDR Banks, and HM3 Nguyen, a dental technician. LCMDR Banks was a tall,

106

medium-built thirty-something-year-old with balding blond hair and brown eyes. He had a light complexion and medium build.

HM3 Nguyen was a Vietnamese American with a light complexion. He was tall as well but had a rather thin build.

We finished our introductions just as the sun was beginning to set. I told HM3 Stokley that I had been up for about thirty-six hours making my decision to volunteer and packing. I asked him if it would be okay for me to get a nap. He told me that would not be a problem.

He informed me that our work schedule would be six A.M. to six P.M. The rest of the time I was free to do whatever I wanted, provided I was not the overnight corpsman on duty. HM3 explained that he, HN Miller, HM2 Smith, and I would rotate that responsibility. So every fourth day I was required to remain at the medical department overnight in the event of a medical emergency.

There was also one more exception to this free time that I quickly picked up on. Whenever there was an announcement over the loudspeaker to the effect of:

"GQ!" (General Quarters)

All hands were required to report to their battle stations for drills. These drills typically lasted three to four hours and occurred several times a week while we were underway. Basically, we worked from six A.M. to ten P.M. most days. Those were long hours, but it helped pass the time and kept us alert.

We were underway sometimes as long as twenty-one days. There was not much else to do on the ship except to work out and play cards and basketball topside. We could also read, write letters and watch the ocean. The ocean really is magnificent, but after a week of seeing nothing but water in all directions, it can become a bit mundane.

As I was stowing my gear and getting ready to hit the rack for some long overdue shut-eye, HN Miller suggested that I take a couple of Meclizine tablets. Meclizine is a little over-the-counter pink pill that counteracts motion sickness. I declined the offer and never lived to regret it.

The next morning I noticed that we kept a bulk-sized, open bottle of Meclizine secured to the wall adjacent to the medical department entryway. Throughout my experience, I observed scores of sailors taking those pills on a daily basis.

Aside from the medical department, the berthing areas and a couple of others, most of the *Kansas City*'s spaces were not air-conditioned. On hotter days, I noticed an influx of sailors reporting to sick bay complaining of seasickness. This was particularly noticeable while we were in the tropic and sub-tropic regions.

We would normally treat these shipmates with a couple of Meclizine tablets, an IV of Ringer's lactate and then send them to their berthing area for a couple of hours. Afterward, they were required to report back to their workstations.

On board our ship we were allotted an hour for lunch and we were allowed to eat as much as we wanted during that time. It never took me the entire hour to eat. I had conditioned myself to eat quickly in boot camp. After ten minutes of two or three trips to the chow line, I was full. I would spend the remainder of my lunch hour either at a

Bible study in the chaplain's office, or topside looking out over the ocean.

My very first lunch break I observed the ocean for the first time. It truly was marvelous. The water was so blue. Of course, I could not see the ocean floor as it was several kilometers deep in some spots; still, it was very beautiful.

After admiring the beauty of it all for a few minutes I looked around. I looked in front of me, behind me and to each side of my sides. All I saw were ocean waves that extended to the horizon in all directions. There were no land masses visible anywhere.

I then looked at the ship from this perspective. I thought how small and insignificant this ship, that I once thought was immense, was in this ocean. My thought process eventually led me to compare myself to it all. I suddenly felt tinier than I had ever felt in my life.

I took my eyes off the sea for a moment and looked up in the sky. I had never seen the heavens so large and commanding before. At that very moment, I prayed and gave God credit for the ocean, the sky and the majesty of it all. I acknowledged that He was in control of my fate as well as the fate of my *Kansas City* shipmates. I thanked Him for this moment of clarity, and I begged Him to keep us safe.

As I mentioned before, I spent my lunch hours spiritually observing the ocean and attending Bible studies in the chaplain's office. CDR (Commander) Daniels was our chaplain. He was a tall, medium-built man with light brown hair and blue eyes. CDR Daniels was in his mid-thirties, and he always spoke in a calm voice.

HN Miller initially invited me to these Bible studies, which were nondenominational. The chaplain's office was very small. Although HN Miller and I continuously invited the other corpsmen to the meetings, they never attended. Eventually, we had to move our Bible studies to the galley as more and more sailors from various departments began to attend them though.

There were several instances where I would meet with CDR Daniels on an individual basis to discuss my drinking escapades with him. While he did not condone drinking, CDR Daniels never once appeared to me to be judgmental. He would first listen to me, and then we would read some scriptures and pray together.

Six days after we left our port in Alameda, California, we could finally see land on our horizon. Pearl Harbor, Hawaii, was the first stop on our West Pac.

On board our ship we wore our dungaree uniforms daily. Dungarees were Navy-issued, bell-bottomed jeans. With these we wore a ball cap that depicted our ship, a denim-colored button-up shirt with a white T-shirt underneath, a black navy-issued belt and a pair of Boon Dockers with black socks. Boon Dockers were a type of Navy-issued black leather boots that reached a sailor's lower calf area.

About an hour before we reached the port we were instructed to change into our dress white uniforms and report topside to stand in formation as we entered Pearl Harbor. I did not mind wearing my dress whites; moreover, I rather preferred them over the dungarees.

The dress whites were made of a combination of soft cotton and polyester. We only wore our dress uniforms during special circumstances. If we were stationed in areas that were seasonal, our dress whites were the ceremonial uniform during the spring and summer months. During the fall and winter months, we wore our dress blues for those occasions.

The dress blues were completely different than the dress whites. They were made of a coarse wool material that made my skin itch. The slacks of the dress whites were designed in the standard dress slacks fashion; in that the fly had a single button and a zipper.

The slacks of the dress blues, on the other hand, were a nightmare. They had about eighteen buttons and no zipper. The buttons began at the sailor's navel and extended sideways and then downward on each thigh to the genital region. We had to plan our restroom visits accordingly. Besides being itchy, the dress blue uniform was very stiff. It was my least favorite military uniform. The dungaree was a distant second.

As we approached the port of Pearl Harbor I was pleasantly surprised at how the water became a much-clearer blue. I was also able to observe dolphins and other marine life swimming just below the surface. A couple of times, a trio of dolphins went airborne alongside our ship. As an animal lover, it was a pleasure for me to see them glide gracefully through the air as they chattered with one another.

As we made our way even closer to the shore I noticed the crowd that had congregated to meet us there. This fanfare was incredible. It was an experience that I had never witnessed before, nor have I ever since. My arrival at Pearl Harbor is a memory that I have never forgotten. I have carried it with me fondly, my entire life.

As we pulled into the harbor I took my first glance at the other ships of my fleet. For the first time I was actually able to realize how relatively small the *Kansas City* was. The other ships had departed California prior to my arrival at the dock. I would liken my impression of the USS *Kansas City* alongside the other ships of the fleet to that of ladybug next to a caterpillar.

We were in Hawaii for two days. I was scheduled for overnight duty on the second night. On the first night I was given a special overnight pass. I was only required to be at my workstation, alert and ready to go, at six o'clock the following morning.

Although there were beaches and mountains to see, I spent my entire time in Hawaii attempting to gain access into Karaoke bars. I was only nineteen years old; and as the legal drinking age in the United States was twenty-one at the time, I was ultimately turned away at the door each time.

The next day I remained on the ship due to my overnight duty obligation. At the time I believed I would visit Hawaii again, many times throughout my lifetime. To this day, I have failed to make that a reality.

After foolishly squandering my time in Hawaii, we set sail for Hong Kong. At the time, Hong Kong was a British commonwealth. A couple of years later, it was officially recognized, once again, as a part of communist China. Hong Kong remains that way to this day.

Our journey to Hong Kong took us about twelve days. At one point we crossed the International Date Line. This imaginary line designates the point on the earth where the sun can first be seen in the sky each morning. Geographically speaking, a new calendar day begins near Japan and gradually works its way to the left; in one hour increments.

Oddly enough, the date and time of day that we crossed it caused us to skip St. Valentine's Day. Our captain informed us we would celebrate it on our way back home in July. It really was not that big of a loss for us. There were only two women on our ship, and they were both commissioned officers. The Navy has a strict no-tolerance policy regarding intimate relations between enlisted and commissioned personnel.

During this time, I had become more and more adjusted toward everyday Navy life. Although I was still a night owl by nature, I was slowly getting used to the six A.M. starts; followed by the lengthy days of sick call and drills.

Eventually, I earned the respect of Lt. Thompson. He allowed me to assess patients, diagnose them, and prescribe and dispense their medications; without his direct authorization. Of course, He and HM1 Reyes were always nearby, if I encountered an ailment which I was unfamiliar with.

This achievement marked a milestone for me. I had learned these skills over a year and a half before. Even then, I was not very comfortable with my mastery of them. My test scores were the result of late-night cramming sessions prior to taking those exams.

Even when we had labs or did mock field exercises, I was nervous and hesitant as a result. I was gun-shy about simple things like drawing someone's blood or even taking their vital signs.

By nature, I have always been a perfectionist to a degree. My ambivalence could have been a direct result of the persistent internal second-guessing of my assessments. This might also explain why I was never much of a dancer. My friends have often told me that I am over analytical most of the time.

As we entered the port in Hong Kong, I noticed right away the difference between it and a Pearl Harbor. There was no fanfare, and the water was dark and murky. Everyone in Hong Kong seemed to be in a hurry.

Hong Kong has a lot of skyscrapers, taxis, factories, and thousands of businessmen scurrying down the streets. From my experience in Hong Kong, I believe that it is a lot like New York City.

During our time in Hong Kong and throughout the first half of our West Pac, my pay was inaccessible. While I was still in Corps School, I had opened up a bank account at the Naval Federal Credit Union in Great Lakes, Illinois. Soon afterward, I began having my paychecks directly deposited to that account.

When I relocated to work in Oakland, my deposits continued to go to the Great Lakes account. This was not an issue, as I was able to make transactions at any ATM that honored Cirrus or Plus accounts. On board the ship was another matter entirely.

Their ATM machine was centralized. Volunteering to join the crew at the last minute, greatly complicated matters for me. This was less than ample time for the disbursing department to update my payroll paperwork. I also failed to contacted my credit union to authorize overseas transactions, so even the local ATMs would not issue currency to me.

This was years before cell phones or the world wide web. Therefore, it was not an issue that could have been rectified in a matter of minutes. As a result, I was on a stringent budget for the first half of my tour, in spite of the fact that the navy issued me small emergency allowances in the meantime.

We were in Hong Kong for three days and luckily for me I did not have duty the entire time. While I was here, I met a Filipino dancer named Christina Reyes. Christina was of medium height and complexion. She had big brown eyes and a voluptuous figure. We began a friendship that lasted, through written correspondence, well after my West Pac ended.

I was infatuated with Christina, who was twenty-six at the time. She told me I was cute but so young. Christina told me that she was too old for me and that her family back in the Philippines had already arranged for her to marry a forty-two-year-old. I was

119

heartbroken, but we still managed to keep a friendly communication line open for months after that.

In addition to spending time with Christina, I also engaged in some drinking and karaoke while I was in Hong Kong. Karaoke in Hong Kong was much different than what it is today. I could not find it in any bars. I found it in restaurants and tea parlors there. I did some Elvis tunes but was surprised to see that all the lyrics were in Mandarin characters. Luckily, I had all the lyrics memorized.

I thrive off of audience feedback, and I did not receive any Hong Kong. In fact, the staff members and patrons seemed to regard me with contempt, as if they did not approve of an American doing karaoke.

They never spoke to me in English. I had to point out my song choices to the video jockey. When it was my turn, he would simply point at me. He called the names of all the other singers. After I was finished singing I received no applause—just empty stares.

Overall, meeting Christina was the highlight of my time in Hong Kong. In spite of my unpopular karaoke performances, the three days in Hong Kong ended too soon. I said my tearful good-bye to Christina, and then we were off to Singapore.

The trip took about four or five days. When we arrived, we dropped anchor a few miles from shore. This was the first time that I did not witness a port-side anchor drop. This was not a problem, as the Singaporean government had privately contracted shuttle boats to pick us up and transport us to shore at no cost to us.

Whenever we went to a foreign port we were given a briefing about the local laws and customs of that particular nation. In Singapore, we were told that chewing gum and littering were illegal. Violations were punishable by imprisonment.

Furthermore, we were told that even if they discovered a pack of gum on our person, he could be locked up. Our Command Master Chief warned us that because the Singaporean police forces were out of the U.S. Navy's jurisdiction; they would not be able to bail us out should we get into trouble here.

With this information, I had a great deal of doubt that I would be able to enjoy myself in Singapore. Apart from the time I spent with Christina, I did not have any fun at all in Hong Kong. I anticipated a far less exhilarating experience in Singapore.

To my wonderful surprise: My reservations turned out to be unfounded! Ultimately, Singapore ranked along with San Antonio as the two places in the world that I would like to visit again—if not move to.

Singapore and Hong Kong were polar opposites. The grass in Singapore was green and well groomed. The sidewalks and streets were spotless and perfectly maintained; with no cracks or potholes.

Although Singapore did not have as many skyscrapers as Hong Kong, they did have a few. They also had a megamall and a central park area. The park was sporadically populated by sculptures and other forms of art. There were hundreds of people taking photographs of this art. Besides taking photographs, many of these people were lying on blankets basking in the sun or having picnics.

There were trash cans everywhere; I observed the citizens utilizing them regularly. At the center of the park was a very nice lagoon that sported ducks and other wildlife. The lagoon offered paddleboat rides for a price.

The currency in Singapore is also referred to as a *dollar*, but the exchange ratio at the time was two to one. In other words, whatever cost one Singapore dollar would cost me two U.S. dollars. As a result of my afore mentioned payroll issues, I was unable to take a ride on the paddleboat.

Off to one side of the lagoon was a small business district. This district included eateries, bars and various other shops— including outdoor vendors. The shopkeepers and customers alike, were very friendly toward me. They even spoke to me in English. This was much different from the reception that I received in Hong Kong.

I stopped in to get something to eat at a pizza shop and was waited on by a young Indian girl. Her name was Ragani. Ragani was short but well proportioned. She had a dark complexion, long black hair and almond-shaped dark brown eyes. Ragani was seventeen years old and stunning to look at. I liked her; and she liked me as well.

We were in Singapore for six days. I was fortunate that one of my shipmates volunteered to work my overnight duty assignment for me, so I was able to spend every evening with Ragani. We talked a lot but were never intimate.

One evening she took me upstairs to a private area of the restaurant and handed me a guitar. We had discussed my singing a bit, so Ragani expressed her desire for a performance. Although I had never been very good at playing the guitar, I had managed to learn a few songs by then.

I attempted to play a couple of numbers for her, but I kept getting distracted by her gaze. Ragani was staring intently into my eyes the entire time. Eventually I gave up and set the guitar down. I then leaned over and kissed her.

Ragani did not pull away. Instead, she pulled me closer. We shared this embrace for what seemed like an eternity. It was electrifying. I could actually feel her heart racing against my chest… although my own heart was doing the same so I might have been mistaken.

Besides spending time with Ragani, I also spent quite a bit of time at Jimmy's. Jimmy's was a small karaoke bar a couple of doors down from the pizzeria. Jimmy's was owned and operated by a Chinese man named Jimmy. He was of average height and had a stocky build. I met him the first night that I was in Singapore.

The Navy had been giving me a meager weekly allowance to cover my expenses until they were able to correct my payroll account. I only had fifty U.S. dollars to spend the entire six days that we were in Singapore. After a couple of four-dollar drinks and half-a-dozen songs, I got up to leave.

Jimmy approached me and asked me where I was going. I explained my predicament to him. I told my new friend that I needed to make my money last for the next five days. Jimmy told me that he

125

owns this bar, and that I am welcome here whether or not I have money. He then poured me another beer and soon after, brought me an appetizer.

The appetizer was coated in maple and brown sugar and generously populated with peanuts. It was very sweet and delicious. The next night I had some more. Eventually, I asked Jimmy what it was called, and he smiled before answering me. He first told me the Mandarin name for it which I quickly forgot. He then told me the English translation—syrup-covered peanuts and minnows!

I took a closer look at my plate and suddenly I could see lifeless little eyeballs gazing up at me. This startled me at first, but I quickly shrugged it off. It was actually quite delicious.

I had an awesome time at Jimmy's. The regular guests treated me like one of the family. A group of them even gave me a ride back to the pier one night.

The week went by very fast. Before I was ready to, I had to say my good-byes once again. I began with Jimmy and his friends. I promised to come back and visit someday.

I spent the rest of the evening with Ragani. Her boss gave her the evening off, so we spent the time walking around the lagoon together hand in hand. I kissed her softly on the lips and promised we would be together again one day. Although we kept in touch for about two years afterward, I never saw her again.

Soon after returning to the ship, we retrieved our anchor and set sail for our next destination—the Middle East. This would be the longest travel time of our tour. We would be underway for about three weeks before we arrived.

During this time, my payroll situation had finally been corrected. I was also a seasoned sailor now. Although I never succumbed to seasickness, walking and carrying out daily functions on board a ship were quite challenging.

The ship rocked twenty-four hours a day. Much of the time one side or the other of the vessel was tilted at such an extreme angle that it was virtually parallel to the ocean. Besides side to side, the ship also rocked forward and backward—all the time!

Everything had to be secured to the walls or decks: medical equipment, chairs and even file cabinets. When you walked, you did not pick up your feet. You just shuffled them from side to side. When you ate, you had to hold your tray down with your forearm, hold your cup in one hand and eat with your free hand.

For much of the time we were alone in the ocean. On rare occasions we could make out the outline of a ship in the horizon around us. One night I went topside to check out the ocean. I could not see it. To avoid revealing our location to enemies, lighting was prohibited.

The sky was filled with stars and boasted a full moon, but this did little to illuminate my path. I could not see my hand in front of my face. I ventured onto the deck about four feet and became suddenly fearful. I was afraid that I might miscalculate my steps and wind up falling overboard. I went back down below and never ventured out there at night again.

By now I had become proficient in immunizations. I took x-rays and developed them. I learned how to properly apply casts and splints. I prepared for and sterilized our surgical equipment; utilizing an autoclave machine. I even ran some medical laboratory tests, evaluated the results and learned how to apply a filling to a tooth!

A couple of areas that I was a failure in were sutures and intravenous injections. I was extremely nervous to begin with; the rocking and rolling ship did not help matters.

I attempted to apply sutures one time. My *victim* was one of our Mess Specialists (MS). These men were our cooks. This unfortunate young man had sliced his thumb open in the kitchen and found his luck tragically getting worse, when he came to me for help.

Everything went great… at first. I properly administered lidocaine to each side of the joint above his cut. This is a type of local anesthesia were an entire area is "blocked" of sensory perception. The only thing left for me to do was to stitch his thumb up.

I could not do it. I poked holes in his thumb and tried to loop the thread with no success. I poked hole after hole. The poor man's thumb began to look like a pin cushion. Thanks to the localized numbness, he was patient with me the entire time.

Eventually, I gave up. Lt. Thompson finished the job for me. That evening at dinner time, I ran into the same cook. He told me that his thumb was in a great deal of pain. He then jokingly threatened to poison my food. I apologized and prescribed him some great pain meds. As I result, I never starved or got sick from his cooking.

About once a week we met up with the other ships to replenish their fuel and supplies. In addition to my sick call responsibilities and occasional overnight duties, I was required to be topside during these replenishments. I was to be on hand and alert in the event of an emergency. We mostly replenished the ships of our own fleet, but on occasion we also replenished Coast Guard vessels and those of the Australian Royal Navy.

We received mail about once every couple of weeks. In spite of this, I actually received more mail during this time than any other during my military career. My mother wrote to me quite often. I also received letters from Cindy, Christina and Ragani.

The night we arrived in the Persian Gulf our captain called for GQ. Once we were assembled he informed us that we would not be receiving any mail this week. He said the helicopter that was in route to deliver the mail to us had been shot down and lost at sea.

He said that at this point our military intelligence was not certain who shot the helicopter down. Looking back, I realize now that might have been propaganda to heighten our senses as we entered hostile waters, but at nineteen years old I was scared to death.

Until that moment, being onboard the ship had seemed like a paid vacation for me. Sure the days were long, but I was getting paid to travel the world! As soon as my Captain made that announcement, reality sank in.

The high school kid who wanted to join the Marines, defeat Saddam Hussein and save the world abandoned me. I no longer wished to be a Marine... or on this ship... or even in the Navy. I wanted to be safe back home, at my mother's house.

We would be in the Persian Gulf for about three months. Luckily, the helicopter incident would turn out to be the only close call for us. Serving my sea duty aboard the USS *Kansas City* had an advantage that quickly became apparent while we were here.

Our ship was docked for ten to twelve days at a time. I was able to go ashore on a daily basis. We would go underway for a day every two weeks to replenish the other ships. Most of these other ships rarely saw land.

I recalled how disappointed I was in San Diego after leaving San Antonio. Having just left Singapore, I was not optimistic about the Middle East. Aside from isolated weekend trips to Bahrain and Oman; and a three-week campaign in Somalia, we spent our entire time in the United Arab Emirates (UAE). We ported in the cities of

Jebel Ali and Abu Dhabi, but I spent most of my time in the nearby city of Dubai.

Some of the customs that we were made aware of here were: greeting someone using your left hand and sitting with the soles of your feet exposed to them were considered insults. Women had to keep their faces covered and were only allowed in public to conduct family business. The only women who were allowed in the bars were the entertainers, most of which were from foreign countries such as the Philippines. It was also considered to be disrespectful for a man to make extended eye contact with a woman who was not his wife.

I spent most of my evenings with a couple of my shipmates at a bar called Garfield's. It was located at a Swiss Plaza Hotel. Swiss Plaza is a hotel chain which boasts numerous locations throughout the world. At the time it had several locations in Dubai.

At Garfield's, the drinks were cheap, the staff hospitable and the crowd was energetic and fun-loving. We mingled with Arabs as well as sailors from both the French and Australian Navies. Everyone spoke English and we always had a blast.

One of the Arabs in particular was a fifty-something-year-old man named Juma. Juma was well off financially, as was evidenced by his gold watches and bracelets. He also had large rings on each of his fingers. Juma was a very generous man who was always buying us beer and appetizers.

The entertainment was provided seven nights a week by an eight-piece band called the Night Hits. They were from the Philippines and always put on a great show. The Night Hits were fronted by three beautiful female lead singers.

Each musical set lasted about an hour and consisted mostly of classic American rock-n-roll and pop music. Occasionally they would sing a number in Tagalog.

My favorite was a song by the Filipino band *Father and Son* called *Miss Na Miss Kita*. The rough English translation tells the story of a man who had a girlfriend whose heart he broke. The girl's heart eventually mends and she is able to find true love in the process. The man later realizes what he so foolishly let go, and that he is now the one with a broken heart.

As a sappy romantic, this song touched me on a deep level. I eventually memorized the Tagalog lyrics, although I did not speak any Tagalog. I would often join the band on stage when they sang it.

The crowd loved it. Besides that song, each night I would sing a couple of other songs. Sometimes a duet; other times a solo. These songs were usually pop music, but occasionally I would do an Elvis number. The crowd preferred the Elvis, especially Juma.

The entire show was always a class act. In the years since that time I have tried many times to locate the Night Hits through the mass media. I expected them to be on world tour by now. I thought a lot of the songs they did sounded better, vocally, than the original. The musicians were top-notch as well. My search results always came up empty, so I am not sure what ultimately became of them.

One of the singers was a twenty-six-year-old named Theresa Leyson. Theresa was short with a slightly athletic build. She had big ears and large, intelligent-looking eyes. She was always crossing her eyes and raising her eyebrows at people as she sang, sometimes at me.

I became deeply infatuated with Theresa. She was friendly toward me, and we even sang a duet together and shared a cocktail on occasion. However, Theresa handled my obvious crush coolly, at best. Of all the girls that I have met in my life, Theresa Leyson is at the top of the list of ones I wish I could have married.

During this time, the *Kansas City* had a policy that if your pay grade was petty officer or higher you could stay out all night without permission. The rest of us had a one A.M. curfew.

One night around midnight at Garfield's my shipmates got ready to go back to our ship. They tried unsuccessfully to get me to go with them. They reminded me of our curfew, but I was having too good of a time to care. Besides, Juma offered to get me back to the ship on time.

My shipmates left without me. At around twelve thirty, Juma and I left the club and headed for the pier. I could not believe how many ships were docked there that night. I could not find the *Kansas City*. Juma was not much help as he had never seen my ship before. We finally found it around three-thirty in the morning.

136

That afternoon I had to stand in front of the captain and explain my actions. Regrettably, I lied. I told him that I had been partying with a petty officer who was intoxicated and did not want to stop partying. I said that instead of leaving my shipmate behind, I elected to remain ashore with him. My deception was satisfactory, and I was let off the hook.

A couple of weeks later, I had to say good-bye to Theresa for the last time. I do not recall a time in my life that I have ever felt that sad. The next day, we began a two-week journey to Phuket, Thailand.

We arrived in Thailand in late June of 1993. We would be here for two days. This was a relaxed port call in that only the sailors who had watch duty had to work. The first night I received special permission to spend the night ashore.

I rented a hotel room, packed two cases of condoms and instructed my shipmates to stop by my room if they needed some. I had not had sexual intercourse the entire West Pac, and I didn't expect Phuket to be any different.

That night I spent the evening at a local karaoke bar. My waitress was named Janpen. Janpen was around my age and was short and petite.

At closing time, I got up to leave. Janpen and a couple of the other waitresses encouraged me to stay with a bottle of Jack Daniel's. We continued to sing together and finished the bottle in about two hours. Afterward, Janpen got up to leave and stumbled into the wall by the door.

I asked her how she was getting home, and she replied:

"My bike."

At the time, mopeds were the predominate source of transportation in Thailand. After a bit of coaxing, I talked Janpen into sharing a taxi with me instead. I promised to have the driver drop her off first, at my expense.

When we arrived at her home, Janpen asked me to spend the night with her. I did not hesitate to accept her invitation. Once inside, Janpen got undressed and climbed in bed. I lay down on the floor, facedown and fully dressed. I must have looked like a frightened puppy.

Janpen turned out the lights and told me I could sleep in bed with her if I liked. I climbed in her bed and within minutes, Janpen had passed out on my chest. I spent the rest of the night feeling her breath and enjoying the comfort that the cuddling afforded.

The next morning; Janpen got up before me, took a shower, returned to the bed and had her way with me. Unfortunately, the two cases of condoms were across town in the hotel room that I rented but did not use. I was paranoid for months after that about sexually transmitted diseases. Luckily, I was clean.

I spent the entire day with Janpen. Once again, I did not report back to my ship in time for my one A.M. curfew. I knew that I would never see Janpen again, so this was far more important to me than that annoying curfew. Besides, I reasoned:

"I am an adult. This is my life; I can make my own decisions!"

I finally said my good-byes to Janpen and gave her my jean jacket. She gave me a photograph of herself and we exchanged addresses. After this, I returned to the *Kansas City*.

The next day we began a ten-day journey for a return visit to Singapore. I wrote Ragani a letter telling her how excited I was to be able to see her again. After this, I had to report to my captain to explain my actions in Thailand.

I used the same excuse that I had in Jebel Ali. This time however, my commanding officer wasn't buying it. He sentenced me to six days of ship restriction and extra duty. Right away I thought this would not be so bad. I reasoned:

"We will be underway for almost two weeks, so what does it matter if I am restricted to the ship for six days?"

My captain promptly deflated my spirits by informing me that I would be serving my sentence when we arrived in Singapore.

When we arrived in Singapore, I spent my days working in sick call and a couple of hours each evening chipping paint topside. I often stared at the city lights across the bay with tears in my eyes. I wanted so bad to be with Ragani.

As we left Singapore, my morale was at an all-time low. I did not seem to understand at the time, that there were consequences for my actions. We were destined for a return trip to Pearl Harbor for our final West Pac stop. I was so angry with my commanding officer that I requested a two-week leave to be effective when we pulled into Hawaii. I had enough of shipboard life.

My request was granted. When we arrived in Hawaii, I said my good-byes to my shipmates and went ashore for the final time. I knew from my previous experience that I would not be able to drink or party while I was in Hawaii, so I promptly booked a flight back to Oakland.

CHAPTER VIII

Back Home to Illinois

I ARRIVED BACK in Oakland on July 25, 1993. It felt great to be permanently back on dry ground again. I was now a much more competent corpsman. My friend Jeff picked me up at the airport and we went to see the first *Jurassic Park*.

Afterward, we went out for a few drinks. I was still underage, but now a confident and experienced drinker. I never had difficulty getting served an alcoholic beverage in California again.

While we were overseas we received extra pay every month. Our pay was also exempt from federal taxes. As a result, I had quite a bit of money in my bank account when I returned to Oak Knoll. I began to spend my money like I was extremely wealthy.

I bought expensive suits, treated my friends to nights out on the town and took long taxi rides in search of karaoke bars. It only took a few weeks for my *nest egg* to dwindle down to almost nothing.

While I was gone, Jeff had moved off base. He invited me to his apartment a few times and told me how nice it was to not have to live in the dorm.

Oak Knoll also had a new addition to the hospital staff. An eighteen-year-old short blonde with blue eyes. Her name was Leah, and she had a light complexion and a thin build. Leah and I hit it off right away. I even snuck into her dorm room several times and spent the night with her. This was against Oak Knoll policy.

About a month later I took my friend Jeff's advice. After talking it over with Leah, we moved off base together. We moved into a two-bedroom, two-bathroom unit at the Camelot apartments.

Camelot was adjacent to the Bay Fair Mall, which was located in San Leandro, California. San Leandro was a town with a population of about thirty-five thousand located about five miles from our base.

The rent was about nine hundred dollars a month. As an E-3, I received four hundred and fifty dollars a month in housing allowance.

As an E-2, Leah received four hundred dollars a month for that purpose. In addition to our housing allowance, we each also received two hundred dollars per month for food cost.

Our housing and food allowances, in addition to our regular pay, should have allowed us to live quite comfortably in spite of the monthly rent and utility obligations. My lifestyle caused me to pay my share of the expenses late almost on a monthly basis, though. This became a point of contention with Leah, who was in the twelve-step program for recovering alcoholics.

Although I was romantically attracted to her, Leah and I did not date. Even when I spent the night in her dorm, our romance only included cuddling and no kissing. We each had separate bedrooms in our apartment, and although I had hoped for and even pursued romance, Leah was not interested.

This may have been in part to my drinking habits. Eventually, Leah began dating a coworker, and he spent the night with her all the time. He was a very nice guy, but I was jealous.

I became increasingly more depressed. I spent every night out on the town drinking and doing Karaoke. I would return home and sing until the wee hours of the morning.

Leah and I had heated arguments about this on a regular basis. During one altercation, Leah threw a broken VCR over my shoulder. The machine had eaten one of my tapes a few nights earlier, and in my drunken attempt to fix the problem, I had destroyed it.

Another point of contention between us was over the contents of our refrigerator. I consistently drank and ate whatever I desired regardless of who purchased those items. Leah protested my selfish behavior a number of times, but I remained inconsiderate.

On October fifteenth of that year, my sister Katy had given birth to her second child, a girl she named Alyssa. I had not even been home to meet her one-year-old sister Nicole yet. On December 7th, at 6:30 A.M., I received a phone call from my supervisor.

He informed me that just a few hours ago, Alyssa had died. She had apparently suffocated in her sleep. This is a well-known condition known as Sudden Infant Death Syndrome (SIDS). I was promptly granted emergency leave and the Navy Relief Organization purchased a round-trip commercial airfare for me.

I arrived home that evening and as could be expected, Katy and her husband John, were distraught. I tried my best to offer them moral support, but seeing my little sister in this state caused me to lose even my own strength.

Over the years I have forgotten much of the details of Alyssa's funeral. Although, I do remember the casket being about the size of a small suitcase. Alyssa looked like a real-life baby doll lying there. She had been born a few weeks prematurely. She was so very tiny.

A bright moment in this otherwise dark time, came in the form of my first meeting with my niece Nicole. I fell for her immediately. At just over a year old she had taken her first steps, but she preferred crawling as her primary mode of transportation. Nicole was my pride and joy.

A couple of days after Alyssa's funeral, I spent some time at my father's house. To be honest, my motivation for going there was actually to drink and party with my friends; not so much to spend time with my family.

At one of our parties, I met a fourteen-year-old named Denise Ramsey. I met her mother and told her that I was in the Navy. Her mother did not believe that a fifteen-year-old could be in the Navy. I told her I was twenty, but she still did not believe me.

Denise and I hung out a few times after this. As I was concerned about the legal consequences based on our age difference, I never even kissed Denise during these meetings.

About a week later, Denise's mother discovered the truth about my age. She was furious. Although she acknowledged my upfront truthfulness and was relieved that her daughter and I had not consummated our relationship, she still refused to let me ever see Denise again. I was heartbroken. I had no plans of entering a sexual relationship with Denise until she was eighteen, but I did like her a lot.

Three days later I returned to Oak Knoll. While I was in Illinois my roommate, Leah, had been given orders for assignment at Naval Hospital Great Lakes. Her assignment was to begin in mid-January.

I called Denise several times, but her voice always seemed distant on the phone... not like it did when we were hanging out. The death of my niece, the impending departure of Leah and the chasm that had developed between Denise and I weighed heavily on my mental state.

Depressed and inspired by my feelings for Denise, I wrote the following lyrics:

Overwhelmed with so much doubt

As I try to figure out

If your love is true

Or what you're all about

Spending all my nights alone

And all my money on the phone

Searching for a way to ask

Has our love grown

Help me to stand

Before I fall apart

Give me your hand

And I will give you my heart

Talk to me

Tell me how you feel

Should I go away

Or is your love for real

By the end of the week, I reported to my LPO that I intended to kill myself. I did not have a concrete plan, but I told him I would if given enough time. My situation caused a problem for the Navy. As

I was a psychiatric technician who happened to work at that location, my supervisors did not feel it would be therapeutic for me to be an inpatient there. They had me transferred to Fort Travis, a nearby air force base.

I spent about a week there getting more and more depressed. My life circumstances were not going to change, and my favorite coping mechanism, alcohol, was not allowed on the ward. I decided to pretend that I was doing much better.

My psychiatrist and I discussed, at length, my alcohol dependency issue. He gave me an ultimatum. If I were to remain in the Navy I would have to successfully complete an inpatient alcohol treatment program.

I asked him if I would still be a psych tech afterward. He told me no. I asked him if I would still be a Corpsman. He told me there would be no guarantees, but I more than likely would be reassigned. I asked him if my discharge would be Honorable. He said it would. I then chose to refuse treatment.

The next day I was discharged from Fort Travis and reassigned to the disbursing department at Oak Knoll. I would work here for the final six weeks of my enlistment. My duties included filing paperwork and running errands.

On February 15, 1994, I was honorably discharged from the Navy. I was very happy at the time. I had never had a job before, so I did not realize how tough life could be without having your rent and groceries paid for by someone else. It did not take me long to regret my decision.

At first I tried to stick it out in California. According to California law at the time, if an individual successfully completed Naval Hospital Corpsman School and worked at least eighteen months on a ward, that individual qualified to take the state LVN exam. California had an identical protocol in place for the state psychiatric technician license.

I got a job as a shift manager at a fast-food restaurant and submitted my paperwork for the psychiatric technician exam. The exam was given once every three months. State-licensed psychiatric technicians were making twenty-five to thirty dollars an hour at the time. In 1994, that was excellent money in spite of the cost of living in California.

Two months after submitting my paperwork, I received a letter of response. I would not be able to take the exam because I had submitted a copy of my letter of recommendation instead of the original. I was encouraged to send them the original copy so I could take the exam during the following cycle in four months.

As a shift manager, I was making six dollars an hour. My rent was nine hundred dollars per month, and Leah had moved out in January. I was already a couple of months behind in rent; I could not wait another four months. Reluctantly, I moved back to Illinois in May. I got a job waiting tables at a pizza place and moved back in with my father.

I spent most of my tips on drinking, which did not sit well with my father. My bedroom was in the basement, and on more than one occasion, Tony would find me passed out on the stairs. Finally, my father told me I needed to find someplace else to live.

At the time, I had begun dating a coworker named Amy. Amy was two inches shorter than me. She had light brown hair, blue eyes, a thin build and a light complexion. We got an apartment together on the other side of town.

Before we began dating, Amy had been living with her former boyfriend's parents. She had dated him for about two years before she met me. Instead of moving all of her things into our apartment right away, Amy did so gradually. She repeatedly spent many hours at his house while I was working.

This made me very jealous. I would get drunk and start screaming at her. I also became destructive. I broke lamps, punched holes in walls and even destroyed the sliding doors to our bedroom closet.

Foolishly, after about three months of this, we agreed that our relationship was worth salvaging. We thought a long-term commitment would solve all of our problems. We decided to get a couple of puppies.

This ended up causing us even more problems. We lived in an upstairs apartment, and although our property manager allowed us to have pets, neither Amy nor I was willing to take our puppies downstairs to do their business. We were also too lazy to clean up after them on a regular basis. My jealousy and violent streak had put a wedge between us. The neglected maintenance of the puppy messes caused our apartment to stink.

We eventually took the dogs to an animal shelter. Amy temporarily moved in with a friend a week later. I became more and more depressed and began to have suicidal thoughts once again. For the second time in my life, I found myself on a mental health ward as a patient.

Amy came to visit me. She told me we could still be friends, but a romantic relationship was not healthy for either of us. During my sobering time on the psych ward, I began to regret my violent actions and jealousy. It was too late for my relationship, though.

After my release, Amy agreed to move back in with me for financial reasons. She had begun dating her ex again, and I reluctantly agreed to allow him to move in as well. Our apartment was a one-bedroom, so they slept there while I slept on the couch.

This was not an emotionally healthy living arrangement for me. Our relationship had been headed down a destructive path. The breakup was the best thing to do; still, I did not want it to end. Each night I cried myself to sleep listening to them make love on the other side of the wall. Soon after this I called my mother and asked if I could move back in with her. She agreed, and I said good-bye to Amy.

I did not live with my mother for very long. My drunken escapades did not please her or my stepfather. To complicate matters, I ran up their long-distance bill talking to friends from California.

One evening Becky aggressively confronted me about the phone bill by pointing her finger in my face. I forcefully grabbed her index finger and pushed it aside. Kenny stepped in and grabbed me. I pushed him an arm's length away and began to punch him in the face.

Brooke and Chad got between us, and Becky called our Aunt Mary. Aunt Mary arrived and talked me into leaving. She told me I could live in her mother's unoccupied home.

I moved into my great-grandmother's house as the sole occupant in the fall of 1995. I went through several jobs but always offered to pay rent. However, Aunt Mary would not accept any rent payments.

That winter, she and I fought all the time over the heat bill. I offered to pay it, but she refused. I would turn the thermostat up and she would come by when I was at work or out partying and turn it back down.

She also had to replace several windows because I had a habit of getting drunk and losing my keys. I would have to break a window to let myself in.

The following January I began college. The U.S. military had a program at the time that honorably discharged veterans who wanted to go to school would receive a monthly allowance to do so. Near the end of the semester, an African American female coworker of mine was at my home visiting me. While she was there my Aunt Mary stopped by. Aunt Mary grew up during the segregated era. The presence of my visitor in her mother's home made my aunt furious. She abruptly left in quite a state, and evicted me the following day.

For the first time in my life, I was homeless. Still, I managed to finish the semester with straight *A*'s and even signed up for summer classes. I took three courses but later dropped out of one of them. I got *A*'s in the other two. I signed up for classes in the fall and again in the spring, but I dropped out both semesters.

Being homeless and going to school was tough to juggle. I was working full time and going to the bars the rest of the time. Some bars were open from six A.M. to one A.M., while others were open from four P.M. until 4 A.M. To keep myself off the streets when I was not at work or school, I lived in the bars.

Quite often a bartender, barmaid, or patron would feel sorry for me and give me a place to crash overnight. I mostly frequented straight bars. However, there was an alternative bar that did Karaoke on Sunday nights. I frequented this one as well.

A former classmate of mine, who was a lesbian, went there too. I would occasionally spend the night with a male patron of this bar. This news got back to Amy and the rest of my hometown.

This was the beginning of gossip that I was a homosexual: To set the record straight: these overnight excursions provided me with a temporary shelter; they had nothing to do with my sexual orientation.

After two unsuccessful attempts at continuing my education, I finally gave up on it. A few months later I met a short, stocky, dark-skinned African American named Latrice Johnson. We met at a Karaoke bar, and although Latrice was twelve years older than I, we hit it off right away.

We spent the night at one of her friend's apartments and ended up staying there for about three weeks. Latrice was married at the time, but had been separated for a few months. She had five kids. Her eldest was only two or three years younger than me.

During this time I learned that Latrice smoked marijuana on a daily basis. This did not bother me at all. I drank alcohol daily; I reasoned that marijuana is not as bad. She also had a rock-cocaine habit.

With Latrice I experimented with *rock* three or four times. The last time we smoked it in a basement. When we ran out I got down on my hands and knees and pushed through the dust and plaster on the floor in a futile attempt to find some more.

When I came down from my high, I realized how pathetic that was. I never smoked rock again after that. Latrice continued to do so though. She didn't do it as often as she smoked weed, but she did so at least once a month. This habit along with my drinking would ultimately become the root of many of our problems.

Latrice's friend eventually kicked us out. We ended up renting the basement of my her husband's house. I was nervous about meeting him in the first place. I was scared that he would kill me.

His name was James and he was a short, dark-skinned African American with a medium build. James was also a Christian who read his Bible daily. In a dysfunctional sort of way, James and I became friends; in spite of the adulterous relationship that I was involved in.

After about six months of living with James, Latrice and I took a Greyhound on a two-day trip to Indianapolis, Indiana. We were both actually looking for a fresh start. We stayed in a cheap hotel room on the eastside of town.

We were impressed with the overall friendliness of the people we met during our visit. We also observed that everywhere we looked there were advertisements for places to rent and help wanted. When we came back to Illinois we decided that we would move to Indianapolis in a couple of months.

A week before we moved, we took Latrice's children school shopping. After hours of shopping we went to an all-you-can-eat buffet. After dinner, we went to a nearby Kroger's to get some groceries.

While there, we got a pack of cigarettes. Latrice was a smoker, and I had been for several years as well. I took the cigarettes off the display and put them in the toddler basket in the front of Latrice's cart. When we approached the dairy section, Latrice placed two gallons of milk where the cigarettes were. I was afraid our smokes would be smashed up, so I threw them in the back of the cart.

We finished our shopping, Latrice paid for our groceries with food stamps and then we went to the customer service desk and asked them to call a taxi for us. They obliged our request and told us it would be about fifteen minutes.

We went outside to wait. As we waited, we each lit up a cigarette. Less than a minute later, a Kroger security guard approached us.

He asked me where we got the cigarettes. I told him we got them inside. He told me we did not pay for them. I said that there must be some kind of mistake. I retrieved our receipt from one of our bags; the cigarettes were not on the receipt. I offered to go in and pay for them, but he was not having it.

161

I tried to reason that if we were going to steal them, then why would we have Kroger's call us a taxi and smoke the stolen merchandise on their property? He told me that he had been watching us since we came in the door and he saw me throw the cigarettes in the back of the cart. He told me I did this to hide them, and he then had me arrested. In reality, he saw a multiracial couple in his store, and he profiled them.

I spent about twenty minutes in lockup and was released with a court appearance set for six weeks later. We were planning our move to Indianapolis in about a week, so I skipped that court appearance. I was also barred from entering Kroger stores ever again. I have never set foot back in that one again, but after several years I began to shop again at other ones. On September 4, 1999, Latrice and I moved to Indianapolis.

CHAPTER IX

The Odd Couple

OUR FIRST COUPLE of months in Indianapolis were rough. We quickly learned that in spite of all the advertisements, not everyone was hiring or renting. I also discovered that Indiana did not share California's policy on military educational transcripts. This was also the case in Illinois. Both Illinois and Indiana required a veteran to go through the educational process again.

Latrice and I paid weekly rentals for a few weeks, moving from place to place; before we were finally able to rent one side of a double, long term. I found an employment opportunity in waiting tables at a family diner.

As Latrice was not working at the time, I worked hard to provide for us. I worked double shifts and sometimes even triple shifts when they were available. As hard as I worked, I partied just as hard. I came home drunk quite a bit. Meanwhile, Latrice continued her rock habit.

Rock cocaine is much different than marijuana. For twenty dollars, a bag of weed will last a single person some time. For twenty dollars, a rock will only last about a minute or two. My income was not shared with Latrice, aside from the little money that I gave her. She still managed, somehow, to support her habit.

Many times I would come home to see a stranger sitting next to her on my couch. Usually, they would leave when I arrived. Latrice and I would have huge arguments afterward. I would accuse her of trading sexual favors for drugs. Her alibi was always:

"We were on the couch smoking."

My retort was:

"I was gone for twelve hours. You could have had sex and stood naked together in front of the washer while it cleaned our sheets and your undergarments."

One night the man did not leave when I told him to. Latrice told him not to worry about me because:

"He ain't nobody."

I told her I'm calling the police. I went to the phone, but before I could dial the number, Latrice came over and ripped the phone out of the wall. I glanced at the handset for a moment, and then I threw it across the room.

It went through the dry wall and fell to the bottom of the wall. I then turned to the man and said:

"It's obvious I won't be able to let the cops handle this situation. I'll have to take care of it myself."

I proceeded to take two steps toward him before he ran out the door.

A couple of months later it was time to file our taxes. Our entire relationship, Latrice rarely worked. She would always allow me to claim two of her kids on my taxes. By agreement, I would give her half of the return.

This particular year, after giving Latrice her half, I rented a hotel room for us for a week. Throughout the week I rarely spent any time with her. I had planned on breaking up with her afterward, so I took the week to think things through. At the end of the week I ended our relationship.

Latrice promised that if I stayed with her, she would quit smoking rock. This was a promise she had made to me many times before. At this point, I didn't trust her anymore. One of the last things that Latrice said to me was:

"You will live the rest of your life alone."

For the most part, her prediction was correct. That was in 2001. I have been pretty much single ever since I broke up with her.

A few weeks afterward, I got a server job in a steakhouse across the street from the diner. I had been trying to get a job there for about a year and a half. I had over fifteen years of restaurant experience at that point.

It puzzled me why it took them so long to give me an opportunity. I had served in pizza joints, diners and even in ritzy piano bars in four-star hotels. I knew the business well.

The day they hired me I sat and waited for my interview. I watched four people who came in after me go through the interview process and get hired. Just before I got up and left, I was finally given an interview.

I had three interviews with this company before. Each time, I was told that they do not have anything available; but when they do, they will call me. I was angry at this point.

I made up my mind that if they hired these four people, and then told me they have no spots available again, I was going to call corporate on them. Fortunately, this time I was hired. Two months later, I was the only one out of the five new hires still working for them.

About four months after I started working at the steakhouse, I took a second job working at a fast-food restaurant. I worked mornings and was working on the morning of September 11, 2001. The reports about the terrorist attacks on the World Trade Center and on the U.S. Pentagon came in all day long.

My coworkers were in tears, but I continued to say:

"That isn't possible. It is all rumors."

After work, I went to a bar. When I began to watch *CNN* for myself, reality set in for me. I became angry and then sad; then I was scared and then I was even angrier. I then drank for about three days straight. I lost my fast-food job because I did not call in or show for work twice.

After finally sobering up, I went to the Naval Recruiting Office to reenlist. Because of my alcohol-related discharge, they would not accept me. A couple of years later when it became apparent that the U.S. military was planning a return trip to Iraq, I volunteered again. Once again, my request was denied.

I worked at the steakhouse for about six years. I became good friends with a girl named Amanda. I was living in a hotel at the time, but I spent several nights at Amanda and her boyfriend Danny's house.

One night when we arrived, her sister's boyfriend was lying drunk on the couch. When he saw me he said:

"Who the @#% are you?"

I responded in similar fashion and an argument ensued.

Danny intervened by telling me if I did not shut up, I could walk back to my hotel room. Amanda and Danny lived about forty miles away, so I shut my mouth. I stayed up all night drinking beer after beer in complete silence.

The next morning we went on a canoeing trip with the rest of the staff members. Once we arrived at the creek, I knew I was guaranteed a ride home one way or another. With this liberty, I opened my mouth and continued the argument from the night before.

Several coworkers attempted to calm me down, including our bartender, Chris Gilkens. He first tried joking with me, and then he threatened to hit me upside the head with an oar. After his third threat, I said:

"If you are going to hit me, then do it. Stop being a 'baby'."

He unloaded a good one on me that sent me sprawling and covered in blood. I regained my footing and followed Chris up to the wooded area above the beach. Everyone tried to stop me because Chris was three times my size and angry.

I ignored them, and every time I would get close to him, Chris would walk away from me. I kept asking him:

"How could you do this to me? I thought we were friends."

He never answered me; in fact, he remained relatively silent the remainder of the trip.

While we were paddling back to our starting point, Chris's canoe capsized. Although he only landed in about four feet of water, Chris was petrified. Apparently, Chris did not know how to swim.

A girl named Kelly paddled alongside and helped him into her canoe. She paddled the rest of the way back, while Chris sat motionless and speechless at the back of the canoe. I had always admired Kelly's good looks and wit, but for the first time I was amazed by her physical strength.

The trip back was quite a distance, but she showed no signs of tiring. Years later when I began writing this book, I turned to Kelly for some critical evaluation of the first couple of chapters.

As a staff we also had a regular Friday night and Saturday night hangout. There was a Latin American cocktail server there that I was particularly fond of. Her name was Carmen Mendez.

Carmen was short with a thin build. She had a medium complexion and large, brown olive-shaped eyes. Carmen had long, straight, raven-colored hair when I met her; she later cut it just above the shoulders. It did not matter to me; she was very attractive to me either way. These *loving* feelings were not mutual, but even to this day I long to be around her.

To her credit, Carmen did attempt a friendship with me on several occasions. Every time she was near me, I clammed up. I choked on my words, and I stiffened up anytime she touched my shoulder or gave me a hug.

I would always drink fast when Carmen was around to help calm my nerves. It always backfired. The last time I saw her I called her a whore.

I wish that once in my life I could have been the suave guy instead of being the fool who always had his foot in his mouth. I regret the way I acted around Carmen, but I mostly feel terrible about the last thing I said to her. Looking back, I am glad for her sake that we never dated. It would not have been a healthy relationship.

Not long after meeting Carmen, I met a gentleman by the name of Bob Matheny. Bob was a fifty-six-year-old computer specialist who worked for the Indianapolis Public Schools system. He and I shared a common interest in music. Despite our age difference, we quickly became inseparable on the night scene.

Rumors quickly began to circulate that Bob and I were lovers. This was not the case. Sometimes the remarks and side glances really got to me. Since that time Bob has been everything to me except a lover.

I lost my driver's license in 1995. I still have not recovered it. Bob has provided me with transportation whenever I needed it, a listening ear when I needed to vent, and ultimately, a place to live.

My credit has been so bad that it is very difficult for me to get an apartment on my own. Bob has been my sole confidant over the past decade. He truly is an angel that God put in my path.

Soon after our first meeting I moved out of the hotel and into Bob's home. He gave me a fully furnished bedroom of my own. His only requirement was that I split the utilities and groceries with him and that I paid fifty dollars a week in rent. Later, we also agreed that I would mow the lawn, rake the leaves and shovel the snow.

A few months after I moved in, Bob's fifteen-year-old Pomeranian named Gizmo passed away. A couple of weeks later I got a six-week-old chow-shepherd mix that I named Meijca. Her name was created by using the first initials of all my nieces and nephews at the time. For Bob, it must have been bittersweet to have another puppy in the house so soon after Gizmo.

Bob was an avid gambler. Pull tabs, scratch offs, state lotteries and daily pools were all activities that bided his time between his trips to Las Vegas (his ultimate passion). After a couple of years of talking about it, he finally convinced me to go with him. I had been all over the world, so Vegas did not seem to be that big of a deal to me.

Two days before we were to depart, Meijca disappeared from our backyard. I was distraught. I could not eat or sleep. I searched for her and called her name constantly. I even left the back door open all day and night.

I told Bob that if my *baby* does not come home, I'm not going on the trip. He did his best to act like he understood. Four hours before our flight, Meijca came prancing through the back door with her tail wagging. We rushed her to the vet for boarding, picked up our friend Abel who was going with us and made it to the airport just in time.

Abel tended bar at the time and was once a coworker of Carmen's. It was also Abel's first trip to Las Vegas. We were both star struck by the spectacle. There truly is always something to do in Las Vegas, day or night. All the customer service employees treat you like royalty. It can be quite the pampering experience. It can also be addictive.

When we returned home, we dropped Abel off and went to pick up Meijca. Her doctor told us she was completely healthy . . . and pregnant. A few months later I was the proud surrogate grandfather to seven healthy puppies.

Meijca had thick, straight blond hair. Her puppies ranged in color from jet-black to calico. The texture of their hair was thick and straight for some and thick and puffy for others. I weaned them myself, making sure they were dewormed and had all their shots.

They were adorable, but quite the handful; especially around mealtime. I researched the proper mix of dry dog food and water based on their age and weight. I even put their meals on three separate paper plates, so each would have a fair chance. They did not need a plate though. I could have just thrown the food on them and the floor, because that is where it ended up anyway.

Not thinking ahead of time I had put my mattress on the floor of my bedroom just before Meijca went into labor. She had the puppies here. Since I did not have proper accommodations for the puppies, they took control of my bedroom while I slept on the couch.

When Bob and I were away at work, we shut them in with their mother; always providing them with food and water. When we returned home, we would hear twenty-eight paws scratching at the bedroom door. When I opened the door I had to dodge seven, twenty-five pound fur balls racing to get out at once.

After their series of shots was finished and they were completely independent of engineered meals, I found each of them a good home. Each good-bye was very painful for me.

CHAPTER X

Sobriety at Last

A YEAR AFTER the puppies, Bob and I planned another Vegas trip. We invited Abel along, but he chose not to go. A month before the trip, I caught Meijca jumping the fence. I learned from experience that she was in heat again. Reluctantly, I took her and had her spayed. I had just raised seven kids; I was not ready to go through it all again—as *magical* of an experience as it turned out to be.

From this point on, Bob and I went on at least two Vegas trips every year. I rarely had any money in my bank account. I would save up for a trip and spend it all in the three or four days I was there.

By now, I had quit my server job, to mix drinks at a sports bar. Although my bank account was perpetually empty, I made great money on a nightly basis. This allowed me to keep up on my bills.

After tending bar for four years, my general manager relocated to Minneapolis to be with her terminally ill father. Her replacement was a tall, fat, bald guy named Grimmie who was covered in tattoos.

One of Grimmie's first acts as general manager was to hire his girlfriend to bartend with me. They attempted to keep their relationship a secret but failed. Their failure was due in part to Grimmie's cocky attitude. He once said:

"I'm the general manager; I can do whatever the @#% I want!"

His girlfriend was a short, petite, narcotic addict named Linda. Linda's hiring created a lot of problems for me. In the best-case scenario, my income was cut in half because I was required to split my tips with her.

I disputed her job assignment with Grimmie. I told him I had been able to handle the job by myself for four years without a guest complaint. My concern fell on deaf ears; he was the general manager and whatever he said was law.

The best-case scenario never happened. Linda had a habit of coming to work too messed up to perform. She would be falling all over the place. She would rest in the office for half the shift and I would still be required to share my tips with her.

Linda was in this condition over half of her shifts. When she was not too messed up to perform, my cash drawer seemed to always come up short. I requested to have sole responsibility for the drawer, citing my flawless past record. Grimmie told me if I could not work with Linda on the drawer, then he would have to find a bartender who could.

A few nights later, Linda fell backward behind the bar. I caught her before she banged her head on the floor. I carried her to the office where she remained until Grimmie finished his shift. He was the swing shift manager that night. He clocked out and escorted her out the back door, allegedly to give her a ride home.

The next night I was scheduled two hours after Grimmie and Linda. Several of my regulars pulled me aside when I arrived. They told me that Grimmie and Linda had talked openly about their romance the night before. They also discussed that they had been involved long before Linda was hired. I became angry to the point that I could not work. I was given permission by Grimmie to take the night off.

The following evening was the NFC championship game. It was also my day off. I came in to have some drinks and watch the game. Grimmie was once again the swing shift manager. At game time he clocked out and also began to drink.

After a few beers and shots I walked up and confronted him. I told him he was robbing me of my income and that he was in violation of company policy by having an intimate relationship with a subordinate employee.

I also told him that this relationship had caused him to show favoritism to that employee. Grimmie stood up and offered to take me outside and 'beat me up'. The acting manager separated us before things escalated further and escorted Grimmie off the property.

The next day I was suspended for a week. Afterward, I was fired. A month later, Grimmie was terminated and soon afterward, Linda was as well.

Three months later, Linda struck and killed a construction worker while she was under the influence. She also had her three-year-old daughter in the car with her at the time. Thankfully, her daughter was unharmed during the accident. Upon her arrest, it was discovered that she had an outstanding warrant for theft. This confirmed my suspicion regarding my cash shortages.

Almost a year after the tragic death of the construction worker, Linda was found guilty and received a twelve-year sentence with two of those years suspended. She will spend the next six years in prison and the following four on work release. During this time, she will be allowed to leave lockup only to go to work, provided she has a job.

Losing my steady job of four years created a great deal of stress between Bob and me. I took a server job but was dissatisfied with my income. It was substantially lower than what I had been accustomed to. After three weeks, I showed up to work drunk and was terminated.

I spent the next three months unsuccessful in my pursuit of employment. During this time, Bob covered the bills and supported my drinking habit. Still, financial tensions increased between us. It was during this period that I decided to write this autobiography.

That summer the U.S. government introduced the Veteran's Retraining Assistance Program (VRAP), which offered unemployed, honorably discharged veterans who were at least thirty-five years old, a monthly allowance to go back to college for one year. I signed up and was accepted into the program. I enrolled in the computer information systems program.

The monthly income allowed me to finally pull my own weight in regards to the monthly bills, but I continued to drink heavily. This drastically affected my studies. I passed three of my four courses in spite of this.

Although I was now able to pay my current bills, those that had accumulated over the previous six months remained outstanding. I chose to drink instead of honoring my obligations. This resulted in many drunken arguments with Bob. Ironically during this time, I also began to get back into studying the Scriptures; particularly end-time prophecy.

I discovered that in the Book of Daniel there are four mysterious beasts mentioned: a lion, a bear, a four-headed leopard and a terrible beast with iron teeth. I noticed that these four beasts had a total of seven heads.

I compared this to the seven-headed beast that arises out of the sea in Revelation. This beast is described as having the feet of a bear, the mouth of a lion, and looking like a leopard. Although I was drunk most of the time, the Holy Spirit revealed to me that the beast of Revelation is the demonic power behind the four beasts of Daniel.

Further research revealed more information about the four beasts. Each represented a world power. The lion represented the Babylonian empire.

The bear was depicted as leaning on one side. This represented the Medes and Persians who conquered Babylon. The leaning symbolized the lack of balance in power between the two empires. History acknowledges that the Persians were much stronger than the Medes.

The leopard represented the Empire of Greece which subdued the Medes and Persians. Upon the death of Alexander the Great, the empire was divided among his four generals. This was illustrated by the four heads of the leopard. The terrible beast with iron teeth represented the Roman Empire.

I also discovered the "Prophecy of the Popes," by St. Malachy. This prophecy, which was written in the twelfth century, gave a cryptic description of the remaining one hundred twelve popes before the end of time. For many, the descriptions were dead-on-accurate up unto Pope Benedict XVI, who was the one hundred eleventh.

I also learned that in 1929, the Holy See and the Italian government signed the Lateran Treaty. This treaty officially recognized Vatican City as an independent and sovereign nation. Pope Pius XI became the first king of Vatican City.

I compared this information with Scriptures. In Revelation, it says there will be seven kings who rule from the great city that sits upon seven hills before the end of times. Vatican City sits upon seven hills.

Revelation also states this monarchy will be dressed in purple and scarlet. These are the exact colors worn by Roman Catholic prelates and cardinals. The chapter says this kingdom will be drunk with the blood of the saints. The Inquisition, a Roman Catholic institution, was responsible for the deaths of tens of millions of Christians.

Combining my sources, all signs pointed to Vatican City being the kingdom of Revelation: Pius XI was followed by Pius XII, John XXIII, Paul VI, John Paul I, John Paul II, and Benedict XVI. Seven total kings since the Lateran Treaty was signed.

On February 11, 2013, Pope Benedict XVI announced he would retire on the 28th. I feared the beast would be his successor. I knew the beast could not take over until after he is released from the bottomless pit. This will not occur until after the fifth trumpet has sounded. I reasoned that the first four trumpets would have to sound during the reign of Pope Benedict XVI.

At this point, I became totally engrossed in current events and Bible prophecy. I could not concentrate on my computer studies. When Pope Francis I was elected and the trumpets had not yet sounded, I did not question God. I questioned my own research.

I studied my findings more thoroughly and discovered a critical error on my part. Although Pope John Paul I was one of the seven popes since the Lateran Treaty, he refused the coronation. He was a pope, but not a king. He refused to go with the flow and was assassinated after only thirty-three days in office.

My current conclusion is that we had four kings, a humble pastor, and then two more kings. It remains to be seen if Pope Francis I is the seventh king. His humility would point against this notion.

One thing we can be certain of though, Revelation states the reign of the seventh king will be short.

As I mentioned before, throughout my six months of research, I continued to drink heavily. My spirit was deeply troubled by my discoveries so I used liquor to cope, although liquor has long been my excuse to cope with everything. I began to preach my discoveries and warnings on social networks.

Much of the time my posts were while I was drunk. My intentions were sincere, and my message was certain, but my drunkenness destroyed my credibility. This further frustrated me and resulted in my message coming across as hateful, even hostile. For this, I am deeply ashamed.

My friend Abel, who is a strong Christian, openly criticized me on many occasions during this time. We had more than a few public arguments. When it was all said and done, Abel was a source of inspiration for me. He kept me grounded.

My message is the same now, only soberly written. The end times are clearly upon us. The time for repentance and salvation is rapidly coming to a close. The final judgment is at our doorstep.

Upset with myself regarding my corrupt testimony, I drastically increased my consumption of alcohol. I began to drink in a single day what I normally drank in a week. On April 7, 2013, I went out and got hammered.

I came home and argued with Bob. He had long grown tired of my drunken preaching. He was tired of listening to my drunken babble. Bob left and spent the night with his sister. When he returned the next morning he discovered broken dishes, trash all over the floors, and an overturned coffee table. I was the obvious cause of this destruction, but I do not remember doing it.

That night I got even drunker and more destructive. Once again, Bob spent the night with his sister. When he returned the next morning and observed the damage he told me that although he loves me, I needed to find a new place to live.

He also encouraged me to get some psychological help. I agreed with him and told him that he has worked hard his entire life and does not deserve to spend his retirement living like this. We discussed the issue at length, and I voluntarily turned myself in to the Veteran's Hospital. Bob gave me a ride there.

I spent the next week in rehab. I was diagnosed as bipolar and am currently on a mood-stabilizing medication. I will take this medicine daily for the rest of my life. While in rehab, I attended two AA meetings and have every intention of continuing to attend them.

I have sworn off hard liquor and feel a lot better now. Bob has allowed me to continue to be his roommate. Although I cannot erase the damage that I have already done, I am committed to preventing myself from adding to it in the future.

I deeply regret the damage that I have caused, not only Bob, but everyone who I have come in contact with throughout my lifetime. I fear that I have a demon inside me comparable to Mr. Hyde.

Epilogue

AS I WRAP up this project in self-discovery I realize the hardships that Bob and I have endured over the past year reflect my mood as I have revisited the demons of my past. I am confident that I have successfully exorcised those demons and am now at peace with those who have wronged me, as well as with myself.

I understand that Satan is the author of evil. I no longer blame David Gillespie, my mother, my father, my ex-girlfriends, Linda, Grimmie, or anyone else for the wrong I felt they did to me. I now view myself, as well as everyone else, as pawns in Satan's plan to deny us the salvation we have been promised.

My enemy is not mankind. Mankind was created in the image of God. My enemy is not myself, as I am a man. My enemy from the time I was lying in bed at the age of three is Satan. I hereby forgive everyone who has ever wronged me, and I beg for forgiveness for the wrongs I have committed against them.

Ephesians 6:10–18:

"Finally, my brethren, be strong in the Lord, and in the power of His might. Put on the whole armor of God that ye may be able to stand against the wiles of the devil. For we wrestle not against flesh and blood, but against principalities, against powers, against the rulers of darkness of this world, against spiritual wickedness in high places. Wherefore take unto you the whole armor of God that ye may be able to withstand in the evil day, and having done all, to stand. Stand therefore, having your loins girt about with truth, and having on the breastplate of righteousness; and your feet shod with the preparation of the gospel of peace; above all taking the shield of faith, wherewith ye shall be able to quench all the fiery darts of the wicked. And take the helmet of salvation, and the sword of the Spirit, which is the Word of God. Praying always with all prayer and supplication in the Spirit, and watching thereunto with all perseverance and supplication for all the saints . . ." (KJV)

Satan is the father of lies. If you do not know the truth you will be deceived. God judges the hearts of men. A breastplate covers the chest area, which contains the heart. There is no judgment for a righteous heart.

Jesus has called us to spread the Gospel. Stand on the truth that you have learned; this is your faith. A wound to the head symbolizes death. The salvation of Jesus Christ conquers death.

The Word of God is the anchor of it all. It contains the truth, the guideline to living a righteous life and a promise of eternal salvation to those who accept the gift of Jesus Christ and submit their lives to His Lordship. This eternal salvation is the embodiment of our faith.

Study the Word of God day and night. Pray continually. Do not fall asleep in your faith or turn away to worldly desires. My prayers are continually with you and your loved ones. I love you, but more importantly, Jesus loves you; so don't ever think that you are without love.

Love in Christ Jesus,

J. Roger Smith